338.7
Sto
2003

WITHDRAWN

The Story of
J. J. Keller & Associates, Inc.

Publishing & Services • Neenah, Wisconsin

Creation – History – Progress

J. J. Keller & Associates, Inc.
1953 • 50 Years • 2003

50th Anniversary Publication

Copyright 2003 by J. J. Keller & Associates, Inc.

First Printing

All rights reserved. Written permission must be
secured to use or reproduce any part of this book, except for
brief quotations in critical reviews or articles.

Published in Neenah, Wisconsin, U.S.A. by J. J. Keller & Associates, Inc.
Printed in Menasha, Wisconsin, U.S.A. by Banta Book Group

Library of Congress Control Number: 2003101376

ISBN: 1-59042-255-4

Table of Contents

Acknowledgements i

Dedication ii

Introduction iii

Foreward iv

Part I: John J. Keller's Personal History

From Birth to World War II 1

World War II Period 2

Post World War II Period 1946 - 1953 5

Business Period 1953 - 1958 7

Business Period 1958 Forward 10

Career Summation 13

Part II: "From Small Acorns Great Oaks Grow"

Preface 17

Just a Lot of Gumption 19

Jack Keller: No Shortage of Ideas 29

A Desk and a Phone 45

The Boys Enter the Picture 65

The Third Generation 73

Growing Up 83

Product Development 93

Responding to Regulations 103

A Part of the Family 111

Giving Back to the Community 115

The Company Today and in the Future 121

Part III: Supplemental Material

Corporate Organizational Activities 141

Publication, Product and Service Introductions 144

Horizon Club 146

Philanthropic Activities 148

Concluding Remarks 149

Acknowledgements

John J. Keller
Author and
Executive Editor   Part I: John J. Keller's Personal History
                        Part III: Supplemental Material

Marion B. Murvine
Associate Editor   Part I: John J. Keller's Personal History
                        Part III: Supplemental Material

Susan T. Hessel
Author   Part II: "From Small Acorns Great Oaks Grow"

Julie A. Nussbaum
Editor   Part II: "From Small Acorns Great Oaks Grow"

Angela M. Biesecker
Design and Art Direction

James J. Pahl
Photography

Advisors
Robert L. Keller
James J. Keller

Development Team
Angela M. Biesecker
John K. Breese
Deanna M. DeVooght
Candy S. Luce
Marion B. Murvine
Julie A. Nussbaum
James J. Pahl

Dedication

Ethel D. Keller is my first associate and my lifetime partner through ten years of marriage at the time of company founding, plus fifty years beyond with the company's 50th anniversary in 2003.

Ethel provided me with three sons — Bob Keller, President (Chief Executive Officer); Jim Keller, Executive Vice President (Chief Operating Officer); and Tom Keller who is presently on permanent disability from the company after years of employment and military service.

It could be added that Ethel and I also have several grandchildren active in the company — Marne Keller-Krikava, Corporate Strategic Planning Manager; Rustin Keller, Internet Product Manager; and Brian Keller, Programmer, and his wife, Melissa Keller, Printed Publications Training & Program Specialist.

Further, Ethel has served as a member of the Board of Directors and an executive officer of the company since incorporation to date. In the 1970s, she established our present Research & Technical Library which is a leading technical library within its field of activity — truly an accomplishment.

Throughout our sixty-year marriage, Ethel has provided great personal support. For example, during our formative years, Ethel and I dedicated all of our personal assets to support the company. With my extensive travel activities at the time, Ethel handled the family and business entirely. Therefore, there is no greater tribute we can grant than dedication of this corporate chronicle to her credit.

John J. Keller

John J. Keller
Founder & Chairman

Introduction

During 2001, Bob Keller, Jim Keller, and Mary Murvine decided to "twist my arm" to consider development of sufficient data and details to create an appropriate company and corporate publication adequately outlining and reporting our very successful fifty-year experience. I agreed with this request and stated that I would not only comply but would act as Executive Editor accordingly.

Following this decision, the group contacted a serious professional writer, Sue Hessel, to handle the story portion of the publication. The author proceeded with her assignment after which the preliminary draft was given to me for review. Simultaneously, I initiated action to develop sufficient structure around the story itself.

Our total corporate experience is far more than a personal report. Considering the activities and experience required prior to company establishment plus the overall activities involved since inception, a detailed publication was the only true answer for presenting the total picture desired.

Considering our impact and position within the industry, it is our desire to be informative regarding not only the company activities but representative of the talented contributions of the overall associate team.

John J. Keller
John J. Keller
Founder & Chairman

Foreward

Being the creator and founder of the subject organization and with the following fifty-year experience reported in this publication, it is only logical that the readers and observers know something about the person who put this "dog and pony show" together.

At the time of founding on November 1, 1953, I was thirty-five years old with a very active prior life experience. I had personally enjoyed a reasonable youth and educational background followed by twelve years of administrative experience in the paper industry, mostly involved in transportation and regulatory activities.

During this period, I experienced approximately three and a half years of military service and was honorably discharged as a Master Sergeant Major of the 548th Field Artillery Battalion with several battle stars and awards.

Next came three years experience in the motor carrier industry as general manager and vice president of an international truck line operating throughout the North American continent. During this time, I gained sufficient education and successfully completed the bar exam for practice before the Interstate Commerce Commission (ICC).

At the same time I also acquired several activities that were helpful in future planning; namely, Wisconsin business brokerage and real estate licenses along with business and life insurance permits. Also, I was granted a Wisconsin public warehousing permit. Beyond my full-time work requirements, considerable experience was enjoyed through land development, warehousing establishment, business and real estate activities plus a partnership in a paint and chemical operation.

Resigning my executive position in the transportation field, an operation was formulated involving a service company named J. J. Keller & Associates involving activities within the transportation, warehousing, and insurance fields. The transportation area involved service requirements whereas warehousing involved necessary storage and containment activities satisfying various markets' needs. The insurance activity was important due to the increasing establishment of interstate truck transport wherein interstate permits were involved. In this related field, there was a severe lack of liability insurance services available. To satisfy this requirement, we established sufficient insurance activities to allow various trucking companies adequate coverage without which they would not be able to operate.

The original developments were all very successful over the initial five-year time period. However, due to extreme growth and various conflicts of interest, the insurance activities were sold as was the warehousing operation.

For the first ten years of operation, we enjoyed a so-called commerce practice which allowed clientele service regarding various ICC requirements including operational permit work for the field. To date, we still handle various permit work for clients through our Tax & Safety Services facility.

Although we operated as J. J. Keller & Associates from our 1953 beginning, we did not incorporate until 1958.

From a one-man shop with my first associate being wife, Ethel D. Keller, we've grown consistently from the beginning to a nearly one-thousand person staff, including over nine hundred direct associates, and additional contract and professional associates. Also, from the initial $1,600 in our company bank account, plus a basic $10,000 bank business loan, we have moved forward to the present approximate $160 million per year cash flow for our business. Considering the complexities of our overall operation, it is remarkable that it congealed so well.

It should be noted that our two sons, Bob and Jim, have invested their life careers to the success of the organization. A third son, Tom, was an associate within the organization for a number of years. Following his military service, permanent disability precluded further company activities.

Experiencing sixty-five years of activity involving the paper industry, property management, warehousing, insurance, and transportation (including fifty years of publishing, consulting, and service-related work), I was invited and accepted induction into the International Paper Industry Hall of Fame. This honor not only reflects personal success, but casts a glow on associate activities as well.

It is evident that we as a group have been practical and successful, and without a doubt, we shall continue the operation into the future. I personally will close on a satisfactory note stating that I am very happy and content with our activities and trust that related parties have a similar opinion.

All our associates, professionals, customers, clients, and suppliers are to be congratulated.

God bless us all for a successful future.

John J. Keller

John J. Keller
Founder & Chairman

Part I
John J. Keller's Personal History

From Birth to World War II

I was born on November 9, 1918 in Appleton, Wisconsin (525 North Bates Street) to Marie Hollenback Keller and Louis H. Keller. As customary for that period, all births occurred at the home residence. Hospitals were considered pestholes for complicated fever and infections due to the lack of medical facilities such as antibiotics, etc.

At my birth, a midwife and doctor were present. Coincidentally, a parade was celebrating the World War I Armistice Day. My mother advised me later that a band and parade was held on our street which stopped at noon. The nurse informed her that the Armistice was called off. It was later announced officially as November 11 with the November 9 date being assigned as a so-called "false Armistice." Therefore, I was a world war baby by two days.

Being blind in my right eye, I had some infantile difficulties but otherwise experienced a normal childhood.

School began at Lincoln Public School for kindergarten and first grade. From the second grade through the ninth grade, I attended St. Joseph School in Appleton.

Other siblings were brother Kuno born in 1913, sister Mary born in 1920, and brother George born in 1922. George subsequently died at age eight from heart failure.

My father died at age 54 when I was 14 years old. Therefore, childhood ended abruptly.

For the high school period from 1935 to 1937, I attended Appleton High School. These years were uneventful due to part-time employment and school activities. I graduated in 1937.

After graduation, I entered an apprenticeship for metal work with the Badger Furnace Company in Appleton. When this proved unsatisfactory, I enrolled at the Appleton Business College in 1938. Various part-time jobs were held in the 1938/1939 period. I was offered employment with the Kimberly-Clark Corporation in Neenah, Wisconsin in 1939 which continued through 1950, including my 3½ years of military experience.

At Kimberly-Clark, I experienced entry-level work in the office. After night school for traffic management, I was placed in the Corporate Traffic Division.

The K-C experience was basic to education in transportation, traffic management, and general corporate and industrial activity. I was trained thoroughly in mail service; rail/truck/air transportation; and handling various clerical, administrative, supervisory, and managerial duties. In fact, these combined industrial and military years were excellent basic training for the following executive transportation management activities plus the later industrial, governmental, publishing, consulting, and service work to follow.

World War II Period

In 1939, war clouds were forming in Europe. I was offered employment with Kimberly-Clark Corporation of Neenah either at the Lakeview Mill or the Main Office Mailing Department. Frank J. Sensenbrenner, the corporation's president, personally hired and assigned me to the Corporate Mail Department in the Corporate Traffic Division. I selected this position as an opportunity to observe how the company operated. It was a wise move as it gave me the chance to see how the entire company and industry functioned. Working initially as a mill messenger between the corporate office and local mills and suppliers was a wonderful experience.

Later, I was assigned as a Corporate Mail Clerk. I attended the College of Advanced Traffic extension school through the Wisconsin Technical & Vocational system through 1942 until induction into military service. At the time, I was working in the Corporate Traffic Division as Administrator for Corporate Personnel Travel & Traffic.

World War II developed worldwide after the December 7, 1941 attack on Pearl Harbor in Hawaii. War was declared by Congress with the national military draft established for personnel staffing.

With my father long deceased and an older brother in voluntary army service from 1940, I became eligible for the draft. Being blind in my right eye plus having suffered gunshot wounds from a hunting accident at age 15 (four pellets yet remain in my body), my selection seemed doubtful. However, the war progressed.

As a precaution regarding possible military service, I personally enrolled in the pre-military training unit at Lawrence College in Appleton. Training courses were held each Saturday by the Wisconsin State National Guard Units.

My induction into military service occurred in October 1942 with departure for active duty scheduled for January 1943, whereby I reported to Ft. Snelling, Illinois for indoctrination. In March 1943, I was transferred to Camp McCoy in Wisconsin for personnel screening and assignment. The situation at Camp McCoy was horrible with much confusion and lack of equipment. After a 60-day stay, assignment was made to Ft. Bragg, North Carolina for basic field artillery training.

With the pre-military training at Lawrence College, my Ft. Bragg experience went smoothly. In fact, due to my so-called limited service rating, I was offered an assignment on the Ft. Bragg staff. However, this appeared to be a stagnant, no-win situation and I declined.

In mid 1943, I was assigned to the Boston, Massachusetts area for coast artillery service with the first station being at Ft. Banks, Massachusetts. Shortly thereafter, I was assigned to Ft. Ruckman on a peninsula in the Boston Harbor where I found coast artillery service interesting.

In February 1944, I returned to Wisconsin on leave and married my wife, Ethel D. Courtois, in Appleton on February 19. After this 10-day furlough, I returned to the Boston, Massachusetts area.

In April 1944, I was moved to North Camp Hood, Texas (a field artillery base) with assignment to the 548th Field Artillery Battery, 220th Field Artillery Group. Due to my experience, I was placed in the headquarters battery of the battalion as Administrative Clerk with promotion to Corporal (T-5 Grade).

In October 1944, our unit moved out of Texas to New Jersey and regrouped on a British ship named the Ile-de-France in New York harbor. We crossed the Atlantic Ocean through the Irish Sea landing at Glasgow, Scotland, and later moved to an English base at Foxley on the Welch border for war preparation and training.

England was under air attack. In fact, my hotel was blown away by V-bombs fired from a European base the day after my personal departure from London.

The 548th Battalion was moved from England across the English Channel to Le Havre, France in January 1945, at which time the Battle of the Bulge was underway with the German army holding just north of Paris. Moving toward the front lines took our unit through south Belgium to a south Holland location. In fact, when entering combat, we had one battery in Holland and two batteries firing from the German side.

Once the Battle of the Bulge was over, the Germans retreated east of the Rhine River and the Battle of the Rhine began. Our unit was in action through the Rhine and other battles to the Berlin area. We had General Patton's 3rd Army on our right flank and the British 2nd Army under General Montgomery on our left flank.

Our unit, the 548th Field Artillery Battalion, was assigned to the heavy artillery activities of the 9th Army under General Bill Simpson. We remained with the 9th Army through the active period of the war until after May 8, 1945 when the 9th Army was dissolved. At this point, the Battalion was assigned to the 3rd Army under General George Patton. Incidentally, General Patton was later removed from the 3rd Army command. In mid-1945 after returning from the United States, he was assigned as Commander of the 15th Army which was in its formative stages. Shortly after this assignment, General Patton was killed in central Germany while cruising with his command through a road repair area.

The 9th Army was the first unit to Berlin in April 1945, at which time General Eisenhower met with the Russians and agreed to Russian occupation of Berlin. Our unit moved north to the Baltic Sea area where we captured Wiesmar in May 1945.

The Germans surrendered on May 8, 1945 shortly after Hitler committed suicide along with his mistress and personal staff. During our following occupation period, we were assigned to the Munich area where we operated an axis prison camp with several thousand prisoners to discharge.

At the time I personally wrote the history of the 548th Field Artillery Battalion which was published by a Munich press. During this period, I enjoyed a T-4 Sergeant rank and was promoted to Sergeant Major of the 548th Field Artillery Battalion with the rank of Master Sergeant.

During the spring period of 1946, our unit was moved to Le Havre and embarked on a transport vessel across the Atlantic Ocean to a New Jersey port. From New Jersey, we were moved to Camp McCoy and honorably discharged. While in service, I received battle stars for the Battles of the Rhine River, the Ruhr Pocket, and the Elbe River.

Post World War II Period
1946 – 1953

I was discharged from service and resumed employment with Kimberly-Clark Corporation in Neenah as an Operations Clerk for Freight Rates/Routes & Product Classification. All veterans were advised to take their old positions which the government had assured. In general, combat veterans were considered poor risks due to physical and mental health concerns, and the government military service was noted for granting full discharge to handicapped veterans to avert responsibility for physical and mental disabilities. This situation remains prevalent today with veterans of World War II and the Korean and Vietnam conflicts.

In December 1946 our first son, Bob, was born. At this time, we lived in Appleton with Ethel's family, and I commuted to work activities in Neenah.

Shortly thereafter, property became available in Menasha, Wisconsin. I acquired a plot of land encompassing six lots with a two-level house on the site. Purchasing this property became the start of my business career since I would have five vacant lots to sell and a house to remodel.

The Bartman family of Appleton owned the property. They sold the tract to me on land contract for $6,500 against which I paid $100 per month. Even at that time, this was a very good deal as it allowed us to acquire a fully remodeled house for no cost considering the income from the sale of the five vacant lots within the tract.

To facilitate the Menasha land project, I obtained a real estate license from the State of Wisconsin. I handled these property sales over a period of time, working out of the home at 900 Second Street, Menasha.

Work assignments at Kimberly-Clark progressed with a promotion to lead a newly-established Motor Carrier Regulatory Section which was advisory to the corporation and all mill locations.

K-C also established an air service operation with my personal support. These activities led to the purchase of aircraft and hiring of needed pilots and staff. The first aircraft acquired was stationed at the Oshkosh, Wisconsin airport and was used for various purposes by the corporation.

In June 1948, our second son, Jim, was born. We were still living at our Menasha location at the time of his birth.

Another assignment at K-C involved the development of a disposal system for mill sulfite waste which required truck transportation between the mill sites and the disposal location. A program was developed to use the material as road binder to seal exposed gravel roadways throughout Wisconsin. Prior to the road-binder program, this very toxic material (technically known as sulfite waste liquor) was dumped into the local waterway system which created pollution. Creating the road surface disposal program was not only economical but also served as a terrific improvement to sanitary waste disposal.

During the development of the road binder program, I became acquainted with Fred Kampo, President of Kampo Transit, Inc. of Neenah. Fred operated a fleet of tanker trucks for combined liquid, dairy, and chemical operations. Together, we worked out the road binder program which satisfied both corporate needs and municipal waste requirements in a very satisfactory manner.

Coincidentally, Fred had been alerted through ongoing federal court activities that he should obtain a qualified administrative manager to supervise his interstate operation. As a result of our successful working relationship, Fred offered me a position as General Manager which I subsequently accepted.

In December 1950, I took over as General Manager of Kampo Transit, Inc. At that time we had a tanker truck operation approximating 50 vehicles. I supervised an office staff of four and a driver staff of 60 to cover local, statewide, and interstate commerce.

Having graduated from the College of Advanced Traffic in 1950 after years of extension school attendance, I enrolled in the Green Bay school for interstate commerce law and regulation. This one-year course was a prerequisite to writing the bar exam for Interstate Commerce Commission practice.

I graduated in 1951 and immediately completed and passed the exam in Milwaukee for admission to the Interstate Commerce Commission bar. Following this, I received a certificate to practice for the ICC.

This certification was vital to the operation of Kampo Transit, Inc. As a result, Fred offered me the position of Vice President & General Manager of the corporation effective from 1951 forward, at which time the company had over 100 large liquid transport vehicles in operation.

From 1950 to 1953, I taught in the state night school system for the College of Advanced Traffic. I taught locally in Menasha for one year and over a two-year period in Sheboygan, Wisconsin. All students were employed in professional fields seeking additional technical and professional education. These years of teaching proved to be a great enhancement for the future professional and business activities that were to come.

In July 1953, our third son, Tom, was born.

Throughout this period, trucking and related operations revealed to me the immense need for regulatory assistance. As a result, the idea was conceived to establish an operation on a public basis for offering various regulatory and technical services to the trucking market.

In September 1953, I resigned from Kampo Transit, Inc., and my resignation was accepted.

Business Period
1953 – 1958

With my resignation from Kampo Transit, Inc. from September 30, 1953, my independent business career commenced and a summation of my personal activities is considerable.

- I was still involved with handling the disposition of the five vacant lots in the land parcel off of Second Street in Menasha.

- I owned a 50 percent partnership in the J. K. Paint & Chemical Company with partner, Joe Kolasinski of Menasha. Late in 1954, I decided this involvement was supernumerary and sold my ownership to partner Kolasinski.

- I held a business brokerage and sales license from the State of Wisconsin.

- I held a real estate brokerage and sales license from the State of Wisconsin.

- I held licenses for both casualty and life insurance from the State of Wisconsin.

- I held a notary public permit and seal from the State of Wisconsin which is still effective.

- Active memberships were held in the Benevolent Order of Elks, American Legion, and the Fox River Valley Traffic Club.

- Both Ethel and I were active with various activities involving the Roman Catholic Church through St. Mary's Parish in Menasha.

At the time, we were actively planning the establishment of J. J. Keller & Associates (with inception on November 1, 1953), a company which would offer:

- Transportation services within Wisconsin and the nation.

- Insurance services principally to parties involved with transportation, motor vehicle, liability, cargo, and property coverages.

- Warehousing services offering incidental storage as needed for cargo, equipment, and property.

The need for complex services such as transportation, insurance, and warehousing evolved as motor carriers desired to capitalize on the opportunity to transport goods out of their local area. Up to this time, even if carriers could secure the necessary permits, intermediate and long haul transport was virtually impossible, and insurance was unavailable.

J. J. Keller & Associates not only handled the necessary permits, but offered affordable insurance for equipment and cargo. The insurance was secured through various brokers that I had worked with over the years. We even made arrangements with the local bank to offer financial assistance. Further, there was a large need for cargo warehousing. As a result, Keller offered a unique pioneering service facilitating transportation activities within Wisconsin and the nation.

Beyond the basic services, we established a commerce practice to facilitate my Interstate Commerce Commission license to practice. This operation was called J. J. Keller Commerce Practice, which handled license and permit work for motor transportation on an interstate basis. This tied in nicely to service the professional work that went beyond the offerings of our basic operation. Bear in mind that in many instances, the regulatory work was the sole activity provided. However, in the majority of cases, we functioned in both a commercial and professional capacity for our particular markets.

During July 1953, office space was obtained in the 100 block of West Wisconsin Avenue in Neenah — a one-room office within a local real estate operation. My administrative associate at the time was wife Ethel.

To activate the operation, a business account was set up on November 1, 1953 at the First National Bank in Neenah with a starting amount of $1,600 (a $1,200 bonus payment earned from my past employer and $400 cash).

Realizing that the world economy was somewhat limited with $1,600, I met with First National Bank President Russ Ward, a friend and past banker for recent employers. A business loan was granted in the amount of $10,000 which set our operation off to tackle the world.

Many years later at the opening of a major corporate facility within our operation, Mr. Ward stated to the group present that the $10,000 business loan in 1953 was the best and most productive loan handled by him over his 40-year banking career.

Our large diversified business activity soon became overwhelming with servicing contacts and referrals, both from a business and professional activity level. In fact, we did not do any major advertising until years after our operation was incorporated, when Bob Keller, who was working for the company as a student, wrote our first commercial advertisement.

Concerning the warehousing end of our business, a plan was progressed to acquire old industrial buildings left from expansion projects by their particular owners. We accessed and managed these properties on a percentage-lease basis which did not require any capital involvement on our part. Over a period of years, we acquired and utilized over one million square feet of space within this program which was both business friendly and profitable.

In fact, during this period, Mayor Richard Daley of Chicago heard of our program and contacted me personally to determine if we were willing to handle the enormous Navy Pier operation offshore Chicago on the same basis. I personally met with Mayor Daley in Chicago to tour the facility and gently demurred from the project, as it appeared overly complex and diverse from our particular operation — although it was heartening to be considered.

Beyond the so-called corporate activity, I was still active within the property market, having established the Keller Park development, a 200-acre project located within the Grand Chute area west of Appleton. This development involved both commercial and residential activities.

To update personal living activities, my family was at 900 Second Street, Menasha, from 1947 through 1955. We moved to County Trunk P in Menasha and stayed there a short three years when a property became available west of Neenah. I purchased a home at 2532 Oakcrest Drive on a two-acre site. I was 39, Ethel was 37, Bob was 12, Jim was 10 and Tom was five at the time, and the business continued to operate in the uptown Neenah location.

Business Period 1958 Forward

The company, founded in 1953, operated on a proprietorship basis. Shortly thereafter, it relocated to 145 West Wisconsin Avenue in Neenah, initially taking an approximate 1,000 square feet of space. The company staff at the time was a president, an executive secretary, an accountant and three technical staffers — a staff of six in all.

The so-called commerce practice was active and brought forward to the new location. Approximately 40 percent of our overall business involved commerce practice activities. From day one, our business was operated on a national scale which created obvious problems but at the same time gave us national prominence overall. In 1958, the company was incorporated as J. J. Keller & Associates, Inc.

At the time, the business was approximately 60 percent service and 40 percent professional. Gradually, we added such items as guides and forms to the line. This resulted in our publishing activities which were handled either in house or through outside vendor services as necessary.

In the 1960s, we acquired some equipment from a small publishing company and converted it to our needs. Through this activity, the operation was moved gradually from a total commercial, regulatory, and service operation to a combined publishing and service operation with whatever professional elements necessary. Meanwhile, business prospered and our staff continued to grow.

The company entered into a lease for the entire building at 145 West Wisconsin Avenue approximating 30,000 square feet overall. Due to our growth, larger parking facilities were necessary. As a result, when an adjacent parking site approximating 50 spaces became available, we purchased the lot from the Kimberly-Clark Corporation.

Beyond the regulatory and service activities in the 1960s, we added the driver's logbook activity to our line plus other regulatory items such as our first publication, the *Exempt Commodities Guide*, which was initially produced on mimeograph equipment. Later in the 1960s, our first major publication, the *Trucking Permit Guide*, was created and sold successfully through its pre-publication period. This guide enjoyed several thousand subscribers shortly after issue.

During the publishing formative period, Bob handled the marketing of the publications, and Jim handled the printing operations utilizing full service printing equipment beyond the office mimeograph stage. Both the boys, Bob and Jim, were active with the business from the start of our publishing period overall.

Needing more production facilities to support our operation, we purchased a land tract west of Neenah in the Town of Vinland approximating 35 acres. Our first plant facility was built in 1971 originally for printing and related operations to support our growing publishing, service, and technical activity.

In the early 1970s, my brother Kuno, a retired military officer living in California, acquired a chemical service company. We agreed to participate and formed the Chemical Service Corporation to further this activity. This company functioned under Bob's direction from a West Wisconsin Avenue location using a staff including son Tom. The operation functioned for approximately three years, when it was disposed of entirely due to pressures from our main operation.

With the advent of adding publishing to the corporation's activities, the business grew to approximately 60 percent publishing, 30 percent service, and 10 percent professional. The professional service was gradually phased out due to conflicts with the overall service operation.

Our basic product line, which included several hundred items in 1970, has grown to over 4,000 items currently. Our staff has grown from two associates in 1953, approximately 20 associates in 1970, approximately 550 associates in 1990, and 950 currently.

The uptown Neenah operation expanded over the full building with a staff of 75 associates. The Vinland operation grew from 40,000 square feet in 1971 to approximately 375,000 square feet in 1990. The addition of the North Park office in 1991 added 120,000 square feet overall. This building turned out to be one of the finest office facilities in Wisconsin. All of the uptown Neenah staff and equipment were moved to the North Park and Vinland facilities which made for a very efficient operation overall.

Much additional land in all directions adjacent to our west Neenah location has been acquired over time through a continual expansion program.

At present, the corporation (J. J. Keller & Associates, Inc.) is the leading publishing and service organization for regulatory, safety, and compliance in North America serving over 250,000 accounts with a staff of 950 associates plus additional contract and professional personnel.

Our operation is the only organization that provides regulatory and legal support to its forms and publications on a continuing basis. Through this activity, those parties using our materials are assured of reasonable consistency. Basically, we are not merely publishers and printers per se as our materials provide reasonable accuracy for the purposes intended.

The corporation operated from the beginning on a so-called associate basis whereby all staff members are considered fully responsible for their activities. All staff members are fully educated and trained for the various work assignments — this dependent upon their particular level of responsibility. The company does not employ common labor as such, as all associates are either educated or trained professionally, administratively, or technically. The only common labor that the company uses is through contract services.

At present, our company is among the top 100 privately-held companies in Wisconsin. To our knowledge we are, if not the only, among the very few debt-free operations which is remarkable considering that our cash flow at present is in the $160 million range. Therefore, the future appears solid, and we have enjoyed consistent growth over the past 50-year period.

The corporation currently functions as an "S" corporation under Wisconsin statutes with approximately 50 persons holding stock in the company comprised of family members, the so-called extended family group, and certain company executives.

J. J. Keller & Associates, Inc. is considered a leader in its field of activity, setting the pace for regulatory and safety publications and services. We are looked upon in the industry and by government as a positive source of information and service concerning our field of activity.

Career Summation
A Summary of Principal Lifetime Activities from Birth to Present

- Served as a Boy Scout from 1930 to 1935, and continue to support scouting to date.

- Served as a Red Cross lifeguard from 1934 to 1938 at the YMCA and at Boy Scout camps.

- Graduated from Appleton High School in 1937.

- Attended Appleton Business College for one year and received certificate in 1938.

- Employed at Kimberly-Clark Corporation from 1939 to December 1950.

- Served in the military from 1942 to 1946. Entered as a Private and discharged as a Master Sergeant Major.

- Attended College of Advanced Traffic Extension Training Program at Appleton and Menasha from 1940 to 1949 (except for three years of military service). Graduated in 1949. Assigned as instructor for Traffic Management and Interstate Commerce Commission Regulation from 1950 to 1964 with night-school classes for adult technical and professional students at Sheboygan and Fox Valley technical schools.

- Passed the Interstate Commerce Commission (ICC) bar exam in 1950 with practice to follow as required. Lifetime member of the ICC and the Association for Transportation Law, Logistics, and Policy from 1950 forward.

- Employed at Kampo Transit, Inc. from 1950 to 1953. Began as General Manager with promotion to Vice President.

- Established J. J. Keller & Associates on November 1, 1953 along with J. J. Keller Commerce Practice.

- Established Keller Development Corporation in 1955.

- Incorporated J. J. Keller & Associates, Inc. in 1958.

- Served as a member of the Board of Directors of Associated Bank in Neenah until age 66.

- Established the Keller Foundation, Ltd. in 1991 for general charitable purposes.

- Established the John J. & Ethel D. Keller Donor-Advised Fund at the Community Foundation for the Fox Valley Region, Inc. in 1994.

- Lifetime member of the American Legion from 1946 to date.

- Lifetime member of the Benevolent and Protective Order of Elks from 1946 to date.

- Inducted into the Paper Industry International Hall of Fame in October 2001.

Part II
"From Small Acorns Great Oaks Grow"

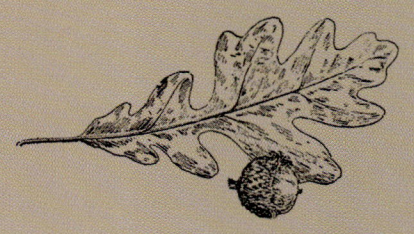

Preface

Considering the history title, "From Small Acorns Great Oaks Grow," it may be stated that this analogy is appropriate. The acorns are the seeds for developing thoughts, processes, and programs within our scope of activities. These resulted in adequate projects for copyrights, patents, and trademarks which were and are the basis for product, publication, and service development. The various items developed from "seedlings" to the "great oaks" of today.

Our present product and service line is comprised of a large group of items dealing with regulatory compliance and safety involving publishing, printing, service, and consulting activities covering manufacturing, business, transportation, professional, and governmental service.

As a completely innovative organization, we have the advantage of being out front in our various markets. We are respected by our clientele and related technical and professional fields as providing not only necessary but essential products and services. Beyond the basic purposes, our offerings are often elementary to favorable expansion and improvement of the users' activities.

From the founding of our operation, we created and implemented the principle to consider each staff associate with responsibilities for work assignments within their area program. Over the past 50 years, this activity has greatly added to the growth and success of J. J. Keller & Associates, Inc.

John J. Keller
Founder & Chairman

Chapter 1

Just a Lot of Gumption

In a time when business was much less businesslike than today, young Jim Keller had his moment of reckoning at the U.S. Post Office in Neenah, Wisconsin. Then in his early 20s but already a young entrepreneur at J. J. Keller & Associates, Inc., Jim had stopped as usual for the morning's mail — at the end of a work week that never really ended.

Arriving in the Keller van, Jim was hopeful that Saturday morning's mail would show a few more orders than the 200 or so the company usually received in a typical week in 1970. His hopes were based on something new that he and his older brother, Bob, had tried in a mailing a couple weeks earlier — stapling an order form to a sample trucker's logbook and to a safety pocketbook sheet. It was doubtful in their minds whether such a mailer would work.

In typical Keller fashion in those wild days of the early 1970s, they had marketed the products without actually having them in hand. Sometimes, in fact, the Keller boys pre-sold products before even creating them. Always, with "just a lot of gumption," they landed on their feet.

On this Saturday morning, Jim chatted a bit with the man behind the post office counter and then asked for the Keller mail. Out came two large mailbags overflowing with letters.

"It can't be ours. It's got to be for K-C," a dumbfounded Jim said, referring to Kimberly-Clark, the Fortune® 500 paper giant founded in Neenah in 1872. No, the bags, each containing hundreds or perhaps thousands of orders, were definitely for Keller. Gulp. Customers had responded to their little marketing test beyond anyone's wildest imagination.

A still stunned Jim loaded the van and drove back to the downtown office, carrying the mailbags up the steep stairs to J. J. Keller & Associates, Inc. Sitting behind a table was his father and company founder, John J. "Jack" Keller. The company was founded in 1953 because no single agency or firm then offered the burgeoning trucking industry the services and products they needed to run their day-to-day operations.

"I turned the mailbags upside down and emptied them all right on the table," Jim recalled. "The envelopes flew all over."

Euphoria about selling so many products quickly turned to stark reality. They were, it seemed, an overnight success potentially on the brink of overnight failure. How would they get those orders out? On their minds was what suddenly became a chilling company promise on their marketing piece: "Order today; we ship tomorrow."

It was standard practice for the Kellers in those days to have no standard practice. They operated the company by the seat of their pants and the sweat of their collective brows. They decided to do what they often did — adjourn the business discussions, which often were heated and prolonged, to tap a few at the nearby Loehning's restaurant and bar. Sitting at the table reserved for them daily, they discussed what they were going to do about these orders.

"After looking at the orders, we knew we had a lot of work that next week. It was definitely a backorder situation," Bob said. "We didn't know what in the heck we were going to do."

Added Jim, "Dad had a plan. He was going to take the money to the bank and we'd figure it out. My job was to get the supplies and equipment — the paper, ink, and the presses."

In the meantime, Bob started calling their new customers,

Loehning's Restaurant in downtown Neenah (current site of Paper City Pub)

Jack's first office was located on the second floor above Barnett's Pharmacy and Schultz Bros. Co. (the fourth window from the right). This building is located at the NW corner of Wisconsin Avenue and Commercial Street in downtown Neenah (current site of BankMutual).

performing a kind of industrial triage, sorting out who had to have product immediately, who could get by with just a box or two, and who could wait.

At that point they were competing with industry giant Moore Business Forms, then the world's largest printer. "It was David versus Goliath," Jim said.

Somehow, the Keller boys always landed on their feet. As Jim put it, "we did the impossible and never turned back."

No one that day would have thought this tiny company operating on a shoestring out of a second floor downtown Neenah office building would grow to 950 associates, a cash flow of nearly $160 million, and a customer base of 250,000. Who could imagine that this company would develop thousands of products, all in response to the needs of business to meet government rules and regulations, or in recent years, evolving workplace safety expectations? Who could have considered the notion that the production division alone would run three shifts around-the-clock and set international printing records?

Keller responded to the trucking industry's growth in the 1950s with much-needed compliance products and services.
(Photo courtesy of Library of Congress: Prints and Photographs Division)

21

The Kellers could. "We were always resourceful. We always set our sights high," said Jim, now executive vice president/chief operating officer. "We like to say, we do the possible today and impossible tomorrow. If it is in our area of expertise, we never back away because of the size of the project."

Bob agreed. "We will do anything any time, as long as we can do it well."

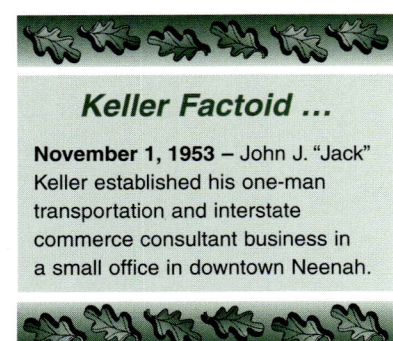

Keller Factoid ...

November 1, 1953 – John J. "Jack" Keller established his one-man transportation and interstate commerce consultant business in a small office in downtown Neenah.

One reason Keller had been so successful with that primitive marketing mailing in 1970 was that it recognized the needs of trucking companies and truckers.

Keller marketed these first products creatively for the time, beating their competition on price in those early days, with a sliding scale dependent on the number of products ordered. A customer could order 100 logbooks or booklets for as little as 30 cents each. A larger order of 500 cost 22 cents each and the price dropped down to 18 cents each for 1,000 — all postpaid. And, 5,000 logbooks or safety books could be ordered for 12 cents each, postpaid.

The Kellers, who were then mimeographing their products, did not expect so many companies to respond to their little offer, including one company in Alaska. "We had no idea how to ship products up there," Bob

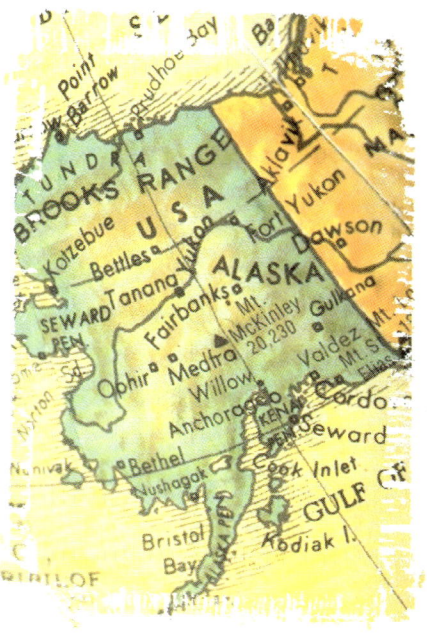

recalled. "Freight was going to top the order unless we could send it book rate which was 12 cents a pound, versus $1 or $2 a pound for regular shipping. But because there was a maximum weight, we couldn't send the whole order."

They contacted the company in Alaska and asked if Keller could ship their order one box each day. The company agreed. For the next 40 days, logbooks went out to places very far north one carton at a time.

The company tested many product ideas in those days, often sending out offers for products based on the benefits they would offer customers. Much like the 12-cent logbook, they sent out offers for goods they had not yet created.

The printing and production department had exceptionally primitive gear. It didn't even have perforation equipment for the logbook printing process. So, instead, indents were made on the pages where that perforation line was supposed to be. "It was years before quality standards arose," Bob said.

Throughout those early years, Keller was a company building the airplane while in flight — something that forced them to be creative in their solutions. They found, as the saying goes, that "honesty is the best policy." When over their heads, they simply called their clients, explained the situation, and came up with a way to meet a firm's immediate needs, hunkering down for long workdays and weeks as needed. "We were resourceful, but honorable," said Bob, now president and chief executive officer.

It is a style that continues today for one of the largest privately-owned companies in Wisconsin and one of the most highly respected in U.S. government circles.

J. J. Keller & Associates, Inc. has grown from a seat-of-the-pants operation to a company that anticipates growth to more than $175 million in cash flow in 2004. In 2001, Keller was ranked the 47th largest privately-owned company in Wisconsin, up in state ranking from 61st largest in 2000. It is thought to be among the very few, if not the only, debt-free operations in the state. It also has tremendous customer loyalty.

Keller's first logo, the "Circle K," was registered with the U.S. Patent and Trademark Office on April 8, 1975. It was first used in 1958.

Keller's current logo, the "Diamond K," was registered with the U.S. Patent and Trademark Office on March 11, 1975. It was first used in 1974.

Founded in 1953, Keller has evolved in 50 years from a simple consulting business based in a one-person office with a phone and a desk to one that creates and markets 4,000-plus products to companies throughout the United States, Canada, and Mexico. More products are in constant development, as Keller responds to and often anticipates client needs.

Assisting the emerging long-haul trucking industry was the impetus for starting the company; however over the years, many more products were developed in these areas:

- Transportation – regulatory references, newsletters, software, forms, training programs, videos, supplies, signs, and labels.
- Hazardous materials – regulatory references, newsletters, software, placards, labels, training products, forms, and other supplies.
- Occupational health and safety – regulatory references, newsletters, and software, as well as safety and training products for forklift drivers, hazard communication, and lockout/tagout.

- Construction – regulatory references, newsletters, software, training products, and work zone safety products.

- Environmental protection – regulatory references, newsletters, software, hazardous waste forms, and spill control products.

- Food safety – food service training products, food manufacturing regulatory references and software, Hazard Analysis and Critical Control Point (HACCP) references, and training products.

- Human resources – recordkeeping software, newsletters, and posters.

- Security – trailer seals, training programs covering load securement and driver safety and security, and reference products.

The story of J. J. Keller & Associates, Inc. is really the story of a company that helps businesses, large and small, deal with the often bewilderingly complex and constantly evolving regulations and issues that affect their operation every single day. Over the years, Keller has demonstrated

Human resources product line

strengths that include recognizing trends and quickly, efficiently, and accurately creating practical and effective product and service solutions.

"Things are changing as we sit here," Bob said.

For example, hot off the presses in mid 2002 — eight months after the terrorist attack on the United States on September 11, 2001 — was a new guidebook, *Bioterrorism: Biological and Chemical Agents Emergency Response Guide*, developed in collaboration with Maximum Compliance Technologies, Inc. That same day, a new catalog was issued featuring a full line of security products designed to protect company assets — people,

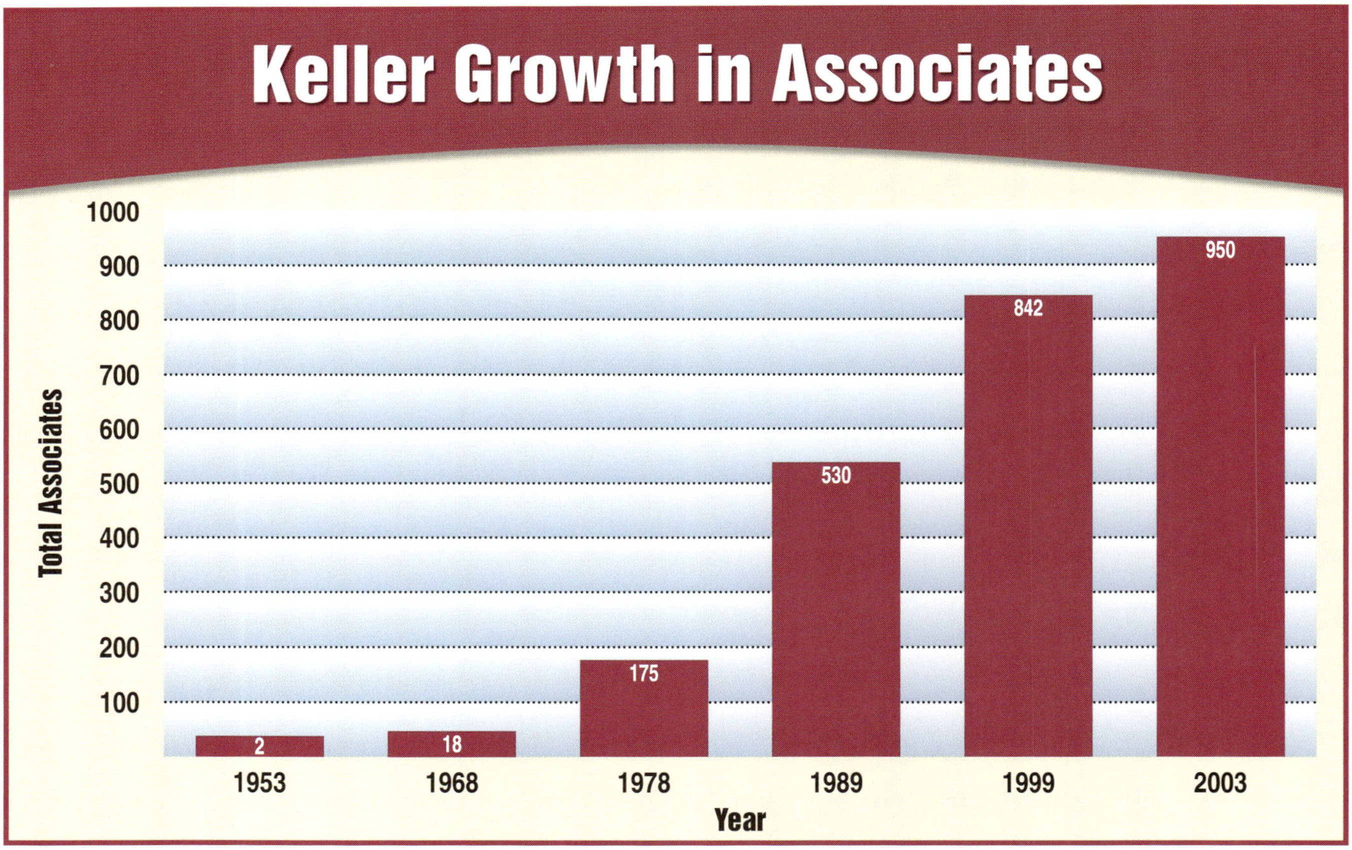

Keller Growth in Associates

Year	Total Associates
1953	2
1968	18
1978	175
1989	530
1999	842
2003	950

property, and information — from all too real threats. Still not done for the day, Keller also introduced a new human resources product line which provides compliance assistance for employers and training and awareness for employees. Additionally, Keller began marketing *Driver Management Online*™, an all-new Internet-based solution for managing driver data.

Driver Management Online™

Today, J. J. Keller & Associates, Inc. has a corporate vision, as many companies do, created after hours and hours of discussions with associates who share their views of what the company should be. After much deliberation, this is the vision they created together:

"Innovative Regulatory and Safety Solutions that Satisfy Needs of all Customer Segments."

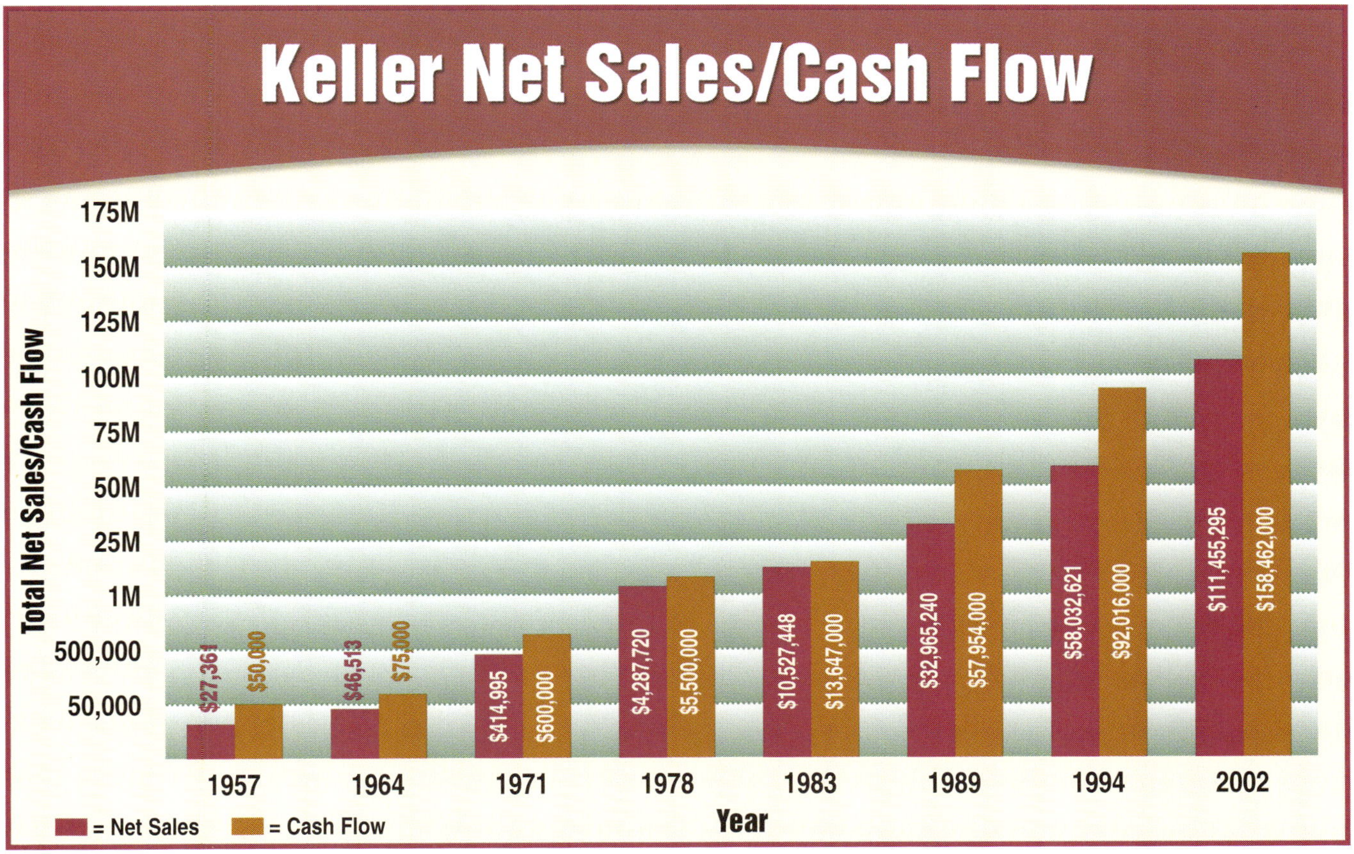

Keller Net Sales/Cash Flow

Year	Net Sales	Cash Flow
1957	$27,361	$50,000
1964	$46,513	$75,000
1971	$414,995	$600,000
1978	$4,287,720	$5,500,000
1983	$10,527,448	$13,647,000
1989	$32,965,240	$57,954,000
1994	$58,032,621	$92,016,000
2002	$111,455,295	$158,462,000

"You could say the vision that dad had was seeing the proliferation of federal and state government regulations in the area of transportation and distribution," Bob said. "I don't think anybody could have envisioned the federal government the way it unfolded, but as a visionary, he could see the way the government would build up in a number of areas."

Keller's purpose is to "identify those opportunities to make it easier for business to deal with government. That is where we compete. That is our reason for being, our purpose, our vision," Bob continued. "We are the best at it. We offer the best value. I don't think anybody comes close to us as far as value and product for the money."

Fifty years earlier, when he founded Keller, the vision was all Jack Keller's — taking advantage of opportunities to create meaning out of a burgeoning government and an increasingly complex regulatory world.

> **Remember when . . .**
>
> ... we had a piece of paper taped to our desks to manually keep track of how many calls we made, how many calls we closed, how many dollars we sold, how many dollars we had per order, and what the running total was — a far cry from the computerization we have today.
>
> ... we all smoked in the office. In fact, most of us had ashtrays the size of hub caps on our desk and had been through the first pack of cigarettes by 9:30 a.m. and the second pack by 1:00 p.m.
>
> – **Dave Ellis**
> **Business Development**

Chapter 2

Jack Keller: No Shortage of Ideas

Let's begin with the notion that Jack Keller is a unique man, a brilliant and a bit eccentric entrepreneur who is a wellspring of ideas that can, have, and still fill filing cabinets bursting with years and years of vision and imagination. Like many of his generation, growing up in the Great Depression was a life-shaping experience.

The son of Marie (Hollenback) Keller and Louis H. Keller, Jack's birth occurred at home at 525 North Bates Street in Appleton, Wisconsin on November 9, 1918. In those days, home births were the norm because, with so little understanding of how disease was spread, hospitals were places where people went to die. If patients weren't dying when they arrived, surely the infections that then ran rampant would do the trick.

As his mother labored, a parade outside their home celebrated what many people thought was the end of World War I. "My mother told me later that a band played and a parade was held on our street, but it stopped at noon. The nurse informed her that the armistice was called off. Armistice Day was later announced officially as November 11 with the November 9 date a so-called 'false Armistice,'" Jack recalled. "I was a World War I baby for two days."

Jack's graduation photo: 1937

It appeared for a number of years that Jack would live a life of easy comfort as his father earned a good living as manager for the Mutual Life Insurance Company of New York's operation based in Appleton. While his dad was highly paid, as the Depression worsened, he loaned his clients money to keep their policies in force when they could not pay their premiums.

Then, in 1932, his father died suddenly at age 54. In addition to the obvious tragedy of losing his father, Jack found at age 14 that he needed to help support his family. The value of his father's estate had dropped dramatically in those dark economic times. Marie Keller lived off residual earnings from the insurance policies his father had sold. It was not enough to care for the family, however, which consisted of older brother, Kuno, who was born in 1913; sister Mary born in 1920; and Jack. A younger brother George, born in 1922, died in 1930 from heart failure.

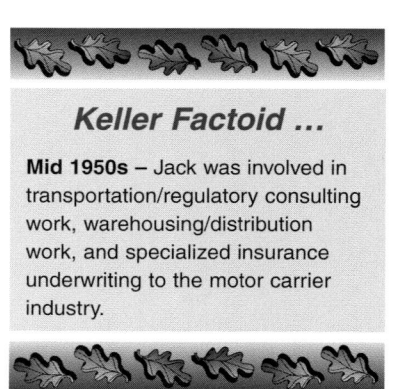

Keller Factoid ...

Mid 1950s – Jack was involved in transportation/regulatory consulting work, warehousing/distribution work, and specialized insurance underwriting to the motor carrier industry.

"Childhood ended abruptly," Jack recalled of his father's death. "I raised myself from age 14 on. I was working, doing it all during the Depression."

Important to the family were his modest earnings of five to six dollars per week from setting pins at the local bowling alley in the basement of the Aid Association for Lutherans (AAL) building, then the tallest building in downtown Appleton. The alley included food service, a non-alcoholic bar, pool tables, and two bowling alleys used by the AAL employees.

"The irony was that I was a Catholic working for a Lutheran establishment at a time when the disparity in religion meant something," Jack recalled.

Jack's education included kindergarten and first grade at Lincoln School, followed by St. Joseph School in Appleton through ninth grade. After graduating from Appleton High School in 1937, Jack spent a summer as a metal work apprentice at the Badger Furnace Company in Appleton. Born blind in his right eye, the job was not a good fit for Jack. "That's when I learned I had no mechanical ability," he said. Jack graduated from Appleton Business College in 1938.

Jack (right) with Hy Redlin at Kimberly-Clark Corporation: 1946

Kimberly-Clark Years:
The Birth of the "Conceptual Man"

Jack was very much aware of the war clouds forming over Europe in 1939, the year Hitler took Czechoslovakia and invaded Poland. With the United States not yet a part of the growing conflict, it was business as usual in this country, particularly at a growing company like Kimberly-Clark.

Frank J. Sensenbrenner, Kimberly-Clark's president, personally hired Jack that year, offering him the choice of working either at the company's

Lakeview Mill or in the corporate office, both located in Neenah. Jack chose the headquarters. "It was a wise move as it gave me the chance to see how the entire company and industry functioned," he recalled.

Jack worked first as a mill messenger between the corporate office and local mills and suppliers. Later, he was named a corporate mail clerk. Unable to afford "regular college," he enrolled in the College of Advanced Traffic, an extension school through the Wisconsin Technical & Vocational System. His experience at Kimberly-Clark led to his gaining expertise and leadership in traffic, a challenging field that involves managing delivery of raw materials as needed in manufacturing and then getting finished products to the customers via a carrier — truck, rail, and express.

> **Remember when . . .**
>
> ... services consisted of only five associates and all the client files fit in five file cabinets. This was when I started at Keller in February 1973.
>
> ... in 1973, services and editorial shared the first mezzanine at the Highway 45 location, and it wasn't even crowded.
>
> – Sharon Kaddatz
> Editorial Resources

Kimberly-Clark's Kotex brand was clearly established by the time Jack joined K-C in 1939, but he would soon have a connection with it through his role in the mailroom of all places. Among his responsibilities was opening mail not addressed to anyone in particular and figuring out where to deliver it.

Jack recognized immediately the potential for Kotex in a letter from an Australian scientist who had a revolutionary concept. Originally, Kotex and other sanitary napkins were attached to sanitary belts that were very uncomfortable. What the Australian scientist sent as a sample was a simple concept — using a sticky tape at each end of the pad that would attach to a woman's "belly and back side."

Kimberly-Clark's development team agreed with Jack that it was worth trying and created a product that it tested with its consumer panel of hundreds of women. Ouch! The results were not good. About 20 percent of the 500 or so women who tested this new pad developed a rash on their skin from the sticky tape.

"We figured damage like that would mean legal troubles. We dropped the concept," Jack recalled.

Years later, this very simple idea came back to haunt Jack in a different form — one that seemed so obvious after the fact. A competitor developed the first successful beltless sanitary napkin that stuck to the panty — not the skin — with stickers on the underside of the pad. "I never forgot that incident," Jack said.

It has been a lifelong lesson. "Now I never pass on an idea. I turn it over and look at the other side. This was a billion dollar idea. Just think, if I had thought of turning it over," he said.

Because of that one experience, Jack became a reservoir of ideas, some immediately applicable and some that needed turning over and over. "That experience made me a conceptual person. Since then, I don't disregard any idea until I look at it inside and out. An idea comes in and maybe doesn't apply to what we are talking about today, but it may be a great idea for what comes later."

Meeting Ethel

Ethel Courtois was working at Wisconsin Bell Telephone as an operator, or what she and her other operator friends jokingly called an "early call girl." Working with her was Jack's sister Mary, who told Ethel she had a brother who would be just right for her. Mary arranged a blind date for Jack and Ethel on April 12, 1942. This was also a double date with Mary and Eddie Gerrits, one of Jack's best friends. The four of them went out for chicken at the West End Tavern in Appleton and dancing at the old Flagstone Club, which had prized entertainment for young folks — a jukebox for dancing. Jack and Ethel hit it off immediately.

Ethel's graduation photo: 1939

Jack and Ethel prior to their marriage

What did Ethel see in this young man? "I liked that he was born with modest means, but felt you didn't have to stay that way. You can change from poverty. I didn't know how, but I knew we could do it together," she said.

Jack described himself in those days as "an industrialist without capital." It meant, quite simply, that he wouldn't let a little matter like not having money keep him from getting rich.

Ethel grew up in Appleton, the daughter of Benedict F. Courtois, a worker at the Tuttle Press Paper Company, and Cecelia A. (O'Halloran) Courtois. She remembered her family as always struggling financially, especially during the Great Depression.

"Everyone in my neighborhood was very poor. At that time, you didn't get food stamps," she recalled. "We would go around the neighborhood and trade food items. This is how we got a balanced diet."

Jack and Ethel's wedding photo: 1944

Ethel once asked one of the Catholic sisters teaching at her school why some people were poor and some people were rich. "She had one word — 'education.' I told her we were so poor, we couldn't afford a dictionary. She told me to go to the public library. So I spent all the time I could from that time on at the public library." Little did she realize how valuable those hours spent in the library would be in the future.

Jack and Ethel were married in the midst of World War II on February 19, 1944, with Jack already in active service in the Boston, Massachusetts area. The newlyweds had only 20 days together during their first three years. Jack came home on furlough for 10 days so they could get married and had another 10-day furlough before shipping out to Europe in 1944.

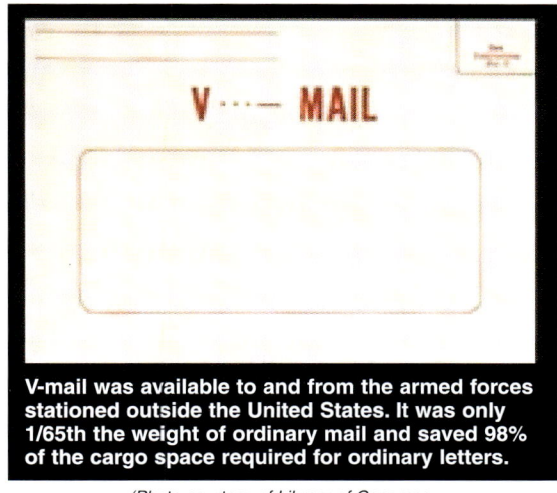

V-mail was available to and from the armed forces stationed outside the United States. It was only 1/65th the weight of ordinary mail and saved 98% of the cargo space required for ordinary letters.

(Photo courtesy of Library of Congress: Prints and Photographs Division)

Jack had sufficient points to be discharged from the Army in April 1946. Wasting no time getting home, he took a freight train from Munich, a two-day trip with 10 men in a cattle car, to Le Havre, France, the city that had been an entry point for his unit into France. Traveling more slowly this time, they landed in Fort Kilmer, New Jersey after about 10 days at sea.

While wives knew that their husbands were soon to be released from military service, communications were much slower and difficult in those years when long distance calls were rare and e-mail was decades from invention. The best form of communication was V (victory) mail, though it took as long as three months to process.

"I didn't know he was on his way home until he hit the States," Ethel said. "I knew he was being discharged, but until he actually called from New Jersey, I didn't know he was coming home.

World War II Service

With his vision problems and having suffered gunshot wounds in a hunting accident at age 15, it was doubtful that Jack would have been drafted — at least early in the war. Jack was certainly eligible for medical deferment and could have spent the war years at Kimberly-Clark, an honorable job during a challenging time in U.S. history. But like many men did then, he wanted active service so he could support his country in a war that everyone knew was noble.

Jack during World War II: 1943

As the war progressed, he enrolled in pre-military training at Lawrence College in Appleton, where he drilled each Saturday with the Wisconsin

Camp McCoy barracks: 1940s
(Photo courtesy of Library of Congress: Prints and Photographs Division)

State National Guard. He was inducted in October 1942, but departed for active duty in January 1943, where his initial training was at Fort Snelling, Illinois followed by 60 days at Camp McCoy, Wisconsin. Jack's basic field artillery training was at Fort Bragg, North Carolina.

By mid 1943, Jack was assigned to a unit searching out German submarines that were sinking U.S. ships just miles off the Boston Harbor shoreline. The coast artillery service was interesting work at both Fort Banks, Massachusetts and later at Fort Ruckman on a peninsula in the Boston Harbor, but he was not satisfied. Jack wanted to get into the real action. After numerous requests, he was reassigned to the newly-formed 548th Field Artillery Battalion and the 220th Field Artillery Group, a unit designed to provide air cover for advancing infantry units. Named the administrative clerk for the unit, Jack was promoted to corporal.

After significant training in the heat of North Camp Hood, Texas the battalion boarded a train on October 31, 1944, for the New York Port of Embarkation. On November 1, they set sail for Europe on the Ile-de-France, an unaccompanied but fast ship that safely arrived in Gurock, Scotland on November 9. For the next three months, the unit trained in England and on the Welsh coast.

When they had a pass, the men traveled to London and other cities, where they saw for themselves the impact the war was having on the day-to-day lives of the British people. "My hotel was blown away by V-bombs fired from a European base the day after my departure from London," Jack said. "It was a hole in the ground. That's all that was left of the hotel where I stayed. I was very happy I left when I did."

In a battalion history that Jack wrote shortly after the war ended, he described the destruction they witnessed as further incentive to fight the enemy. "Visits to bombed out areas in the large cities and the German-launched V-bombs that were landing daily impressed on every soldier that the Germans

Keller Factoid ...

Mid 1960s – Ethel Keller established the Research & Technical Library.

were a fanatical and deadly enemy. Every soldier realized that the United States was very fortunate in not having its cities subjected to direct warfare as were the cities of European nations."

Depending on the battle, the 548th was attached to various units during its roughly 13 months of active war duty. Among actions vital to defeating Germany were the battles of Roer River, Rhine River, Ruhr Pocket and Elbe River. Often, the artillery unit's role was to provide cover to units advancing over those rivers.

Jack recalled on one occasion, the men, remembering an abandoned brewery they'd seen down the road, decided it was time to have a party. They went to the cellar of the building to tap the biggest keg any of them could ever hope to find, taking a sledgehammer to the beer vats.

With a whoosh, thousands of gallons of beer came gushing out and Jack suddenly found himself up to his neck in beer. Managing to survive the brewed flood, they filled five-gallon packs and carried them back to the rest of the men in their unit.

Jack still remembers the officer who looked over these men just after swimming in their river of beer. "We didn't look too good and we smelled something horrible," he recalled.

As the war came to an end in May 1945, Jack described the final days, "Although the official war did not end for days later, it was apparent that the Germans were through fighting on May 3, for all over the sector, thousands of German soldiers laid down their arms and were streaming through Allied lines," he wrote. "Instead of shooting, a big problem developed in directing German soldiers to the Allied Prisoner of War Stockades."

Field artillery units on the move during World War II
(Photos courtesy of Library of Congress: Prints and Photographs Division)

At the time, his unit had been training to be sent to the Pacific. It was close enough to deployment that the men were receiving immunizations needed to protect them from the perilous diseases of the islands. Their orders changed dramatically when the war on Japan ended shortly after the United States dropped atomic bombs on Hiroshima and Nagasaki.

Jack's unit became part of the occupying force in the Munich area of Germany. They ran a prison camp in Bad Abling, about 50 miles from where Hitler had a retreat and supposedly spent his last days. The camp discharged about a million Axis soldiers — Germans, Czechs, and Austrians. Sadly, after living through years of Allied bombings, these prisoners had nowhere to go. Unless they had a ration book, they would starve. "Food was as precious as gold in those days," Jack recalled.

How desperate were the prisoners for food? He told the story of a major asking him for help finding his missing dog. After a search, Jack learned the sad fate of the beloved pup. The prison cook, desperate for meat to feed his men, had created dog stew.

"Any live animal was part of the food," Jack said. "I reported to the major that they ate his dog for lunch. He got angry but said, 'At least he is serving a noble purpose.'"

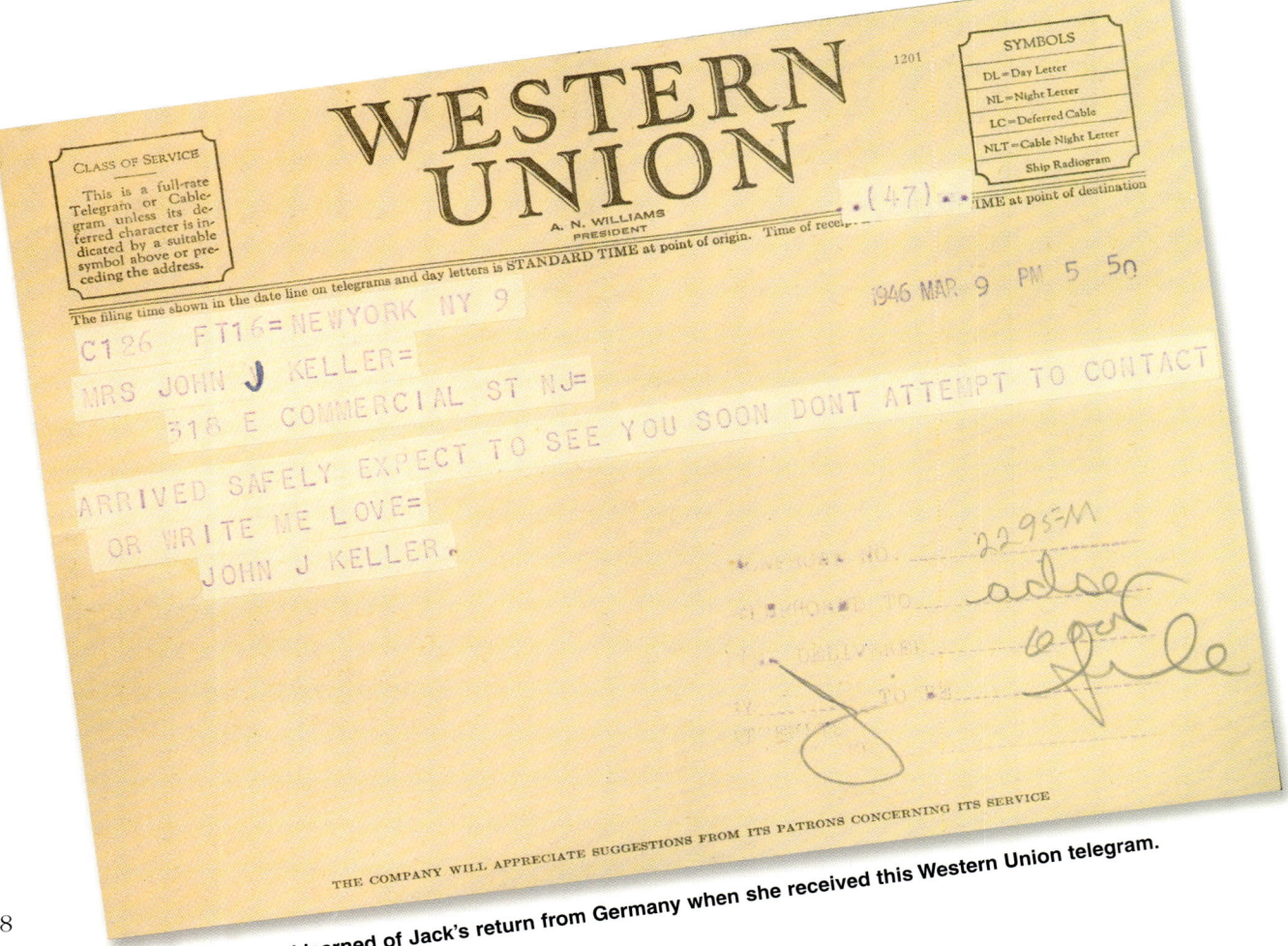

Ethel learned of Jack's return from Germany when she received this Western Union telegram.

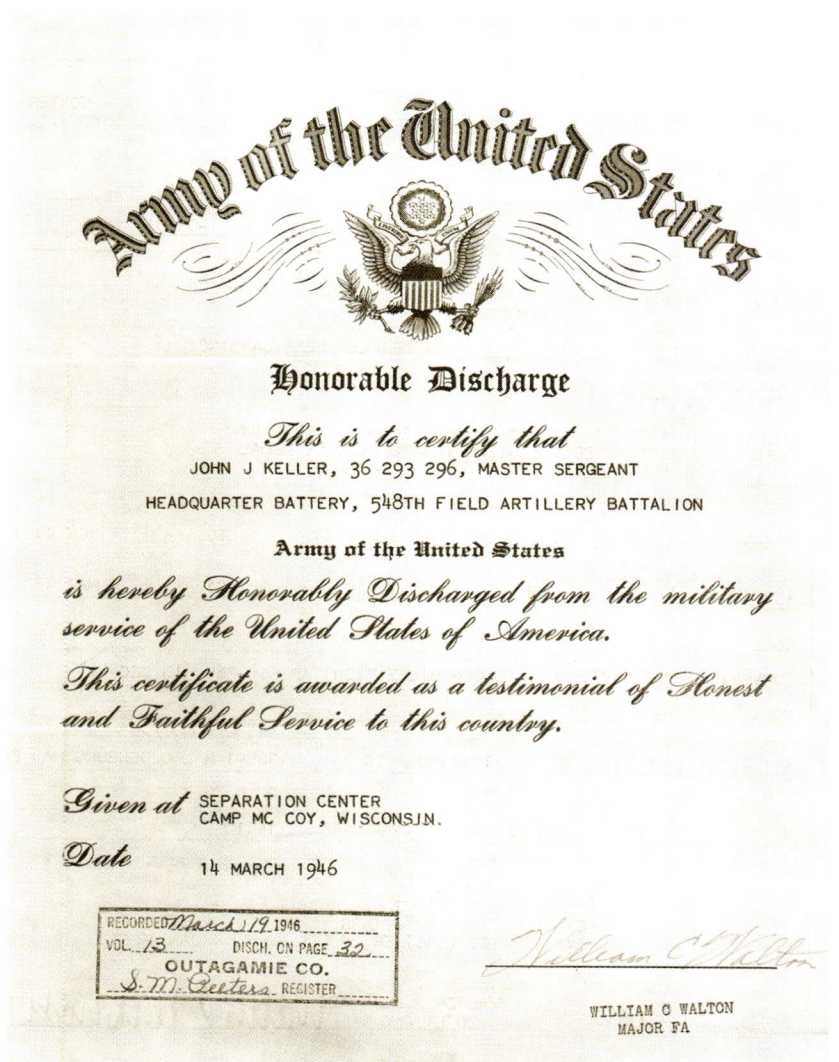

Jack's Honorable Discharge Certificate

Return to Civilian Life

After the war, Jack returned to Kimberly-Clark as an operations clerk for freight rates/routes and product classification. He commuted to work from Appleton, where the family initially lived with Ethel's family. Their first son, Robert Louis, was born in December 1946. James Joseph was born in June 1948, and Thomas Edward, their youngest, would arrive five years later in July 1953.

In 1946, Jack began a start-up company on the side. Operating as Keller Properties, he bought a plot of land in Menasha, Wisconsin with six lots and a two-story house on one of the sites. In addition to remodeling the house for the family, he earned a real estate license so he could sell the other five lots.

Clockwise from top: Bob, Jim, and Tom: 1955

In the meantime, Jack was also working and learning as hard and fast as he could. Among assignments was heading a newly-established Motor Carrier Regulatory Section. He also was involved in the air service operation, encouraging the company to buy its first aircraft in 1948 to transport executives and engineers traveling between the headquarters in Neenah and company mills located throughout the country. Out of that initial service came K-C Aviation in 1969, to refurbish and maintain corporate aircraft. Success of that venture later led to the development of a commercial airline, Midwest Express Airlines, which is based in Milwaukee.

Jack also helped develop a disposal system for mill sulfite waste, also known as sulfite waste liquor, which was transported from mill sites to where it could be disposed. Prior to this new system, the material was dumped into local waterways. The disposal system used the material as road binder to seal exposed gravel roadways throughout the Fox Cities and much of Wisconsin. "Creating the road surface disposal program was not only economical, but also served as a terrific improvement to sanitary waste disposal," Jack said.

Despite his years with Kimberly-Clark, it was not a place where Jack would become rich — except in experience and ideas that he later applied in his own business.

"I started working at K-C for $75 a month," he said. "You don't get rich on $75 a month. When I left K-C, I was making about $375 a month, not even $100 a week. There was no big money in those years. You didn't get rich working. Before World War II, you were lucky enough to have money to pay your bills."

However, the K-C experience taught him a lot about transportation, traffic management, and general corporate and industrial activities, including

Keller Factoid ...

Early 1960s – The *Transportation Journal & Exchange Bulletin* heralded the entrance of Keller into technical publishing for the transportation industry.

mail service, rail/truck/air transportation and handling various clerical, administrative, supervisory, and managerial duties. "In fact, these combined industrial and military years were excellent basic training for the executive transportation management activities and later industrial, governmental, publishing, consulting, and service work that followed," he said.

Kampo Transit

It was while he was working on the road binder program for Kimberly-Clark that Jack met Fred Kampo, president of Kampo Transit, Inc. of Neenah, a company with a fleet of tanker trucks for liquid, dairy, and chemical operations. Needing an administrative manager for his interstate operations, Kampo offered the position of general manager to Jack, which he assumed in December 1950.

Kampo Transit, a company that was purchased by Schneider National in 1969, had a fleet of 50 trucks and 60 operators when Jack started with the company.

Assisting Jack in this work was his education at the College of Advanced Traffic, which he completed in 1950 after years of extension school; and the Green Bay School of Interstate Commerce Law and Regulation, a program that allowed him to write the bar exam for Interstate Commerce Commission practice. He was admitted to the ICC bar in 1951, which allowed him to practice on a national basis.

> **The Interstate Commerce Commission (ICC)**
>
> Federal oversight of the motor carrier industry began in 1935 under the Interstate Commerce Commission. The ICC regulated economic issues such as motor carriers' operating authority, rates and routes, vehicle leasing, and freight claims. It was abolished in 1995 when its regulations were placed under the jurisdiction of the Department of Transportation (DOT).

Even at Kimberly-Clark, Jack already had garnered a reputation as an ideas man, but one with pragmatism. "I worked with a man at K-C who had new ideas every day, but none had any practicality. One day I ran into him and he said, 'Gee, Jack, your stuff generally works out. Tell me how.' I told him you don't have practical reasoning in your ideas. You have to have practicality so your ideas are doable."

Where did these ideas come from? As he puts it, they're "a combination of curiosity and impulse," attributes that are not in short supply in Jack Keller.

"I used my youth and my time at K-C, including my wartime years and time at Kampo as my education process," he said. "A lot of thinking went into my operation and its success before I got into the ring."

Jack resigned from Kampo Transit on September 30, 1953.

Business Enterprises

By the time Jack started J. J. Keller & Associates, he was a busy entrepreneur:

- Owning Keller Properties, his development company, which handled the disposition of the five vacant lots in the land parcel off of Second Street in Menasha.

- Owning 50 percent partnership in the J. K. Paint & Chemical Company with his partner, Joe Kolasinski of Menasha. He sold his share to Joe in 1954.

- Holding business brokerage and sales licenses, real estate brokerage and sales licenses, and casualty and life insurance licenses from the State of Wisconsin.

- Holding a state notary public permit and seal.

Jack had many other business enterprises over the years, including parts of an oil company, a soap company, and a chemical company. He also operated a public warehousing company in the Fox Valley area.

Son Bob recognized that his father was constantly searching for new ideas and new investments. Even Sunday afternoons with the family were designed to combine business with pleasure.

"Dad always followed his nose wherever he got a business venture," Bob said. "On Sunday afternoons, we always went for a ride in the old Nash and we always got stuck. Dad was curious, so he took the back roads, which invariably led us into mud holes. In fact, he kept a shovel and rake in the trunk, just in case."

"Dad was always looking for new business opportunities," Jim said.

"Looking for business at the end of the rainbow," Bob added.

So creative and far thinking was he, Jack stored bricks in the backyard that he had gotten from a company that went out of business. "He said, 'Someday, I may use them to start a business,'" Bob recalled.

> **Remember when . . .**
>
> ... the "great data processing flood" occurred. During a construction project, a water line burst when it was exposed to outside freezing temperatures — spraying water for an unknown amount of time. When discovered, the area looked like a war zone with much of the ceiling collapsed, wires hanging everywhere, and soaked Wang CRTs, furniture, pictures, and documentation manuals.
>
> ... Keller shut down because of a large snowstorm on a Thursday afternoon in January 1978. By Monday morning, the snowplows had come through, leaving eight-foot high walls of snow along County Highway 114.
>
> – Tom Hupf
> **Information Systems**

On another occasion, Jack got 40 chickens in payment on a client's bill. "You wouldn't do business that way today," Jim said.

Always looking for opportunities, there were purchases of ostrich eggs and kangaroo hides from Australia, which he acquired with the thought of going into the import/export business. At one point he considered getting into the barge business, thinking it would be a natural outgrowth of his work with the transportation industry.

Jack took the family for Sunday drives in a 1949 Nash.

Bob remembers the 700 pounds of apples his dad bought because he thought it was a good deal. "The apples went down into the cellar and he forgot about them, and then we got rats and had to go out and buy mousetraps. Then he wanted to invent a new way to catch rats, so he designed a rat solution," Bob said.

Solutions, for rats or humans, were the foundation of Jack's business.

"I'm almost obsessed with my next project all the time," he once told an interviewer. "It's almost like a circus promoter who's concerned with his next show."

The Keller family: 1959

Jack enjoying leisure time while fishing: late 1940s

Chapter 3

A Desk and a Phone

Having worked in traffic for two Wisconsin companies, Jack recognized an industry that was coming into its own. At the start of the 20th century when automobiles, let alone trucks, were a novelty, nearly all shipping was done by rail. The need for a more efficient method was growing, as rail schedules were inflexible and it took what often seemed like forever for either the raw materials or finished product to reach their destinations. Shipment flexibility was limited because the products traveled when and where the trains went.

It was not until the mid 1930s that the U.S. Congress recognized the emerging trucking industry, passing the Motor Carrier Act in 1935.

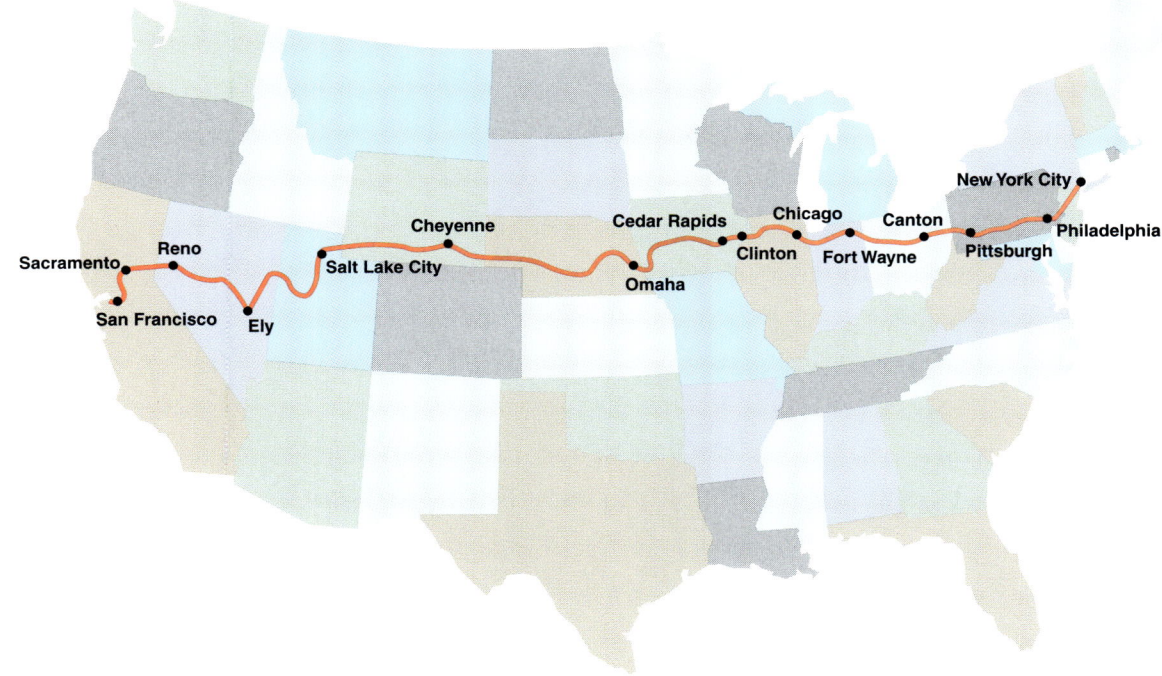

The Lincoln Highway was America's first transcontinental highway, paving the way for the development of a nationwide highway network.

The Interstate Commerce Commission (ICC), the first regulatory commission in the United States, had been created in the 1880s following public outrage over railroad industry abuses. The outrage focused on monopolies and what was perceived as excessive charges — simply because customers had no other options. The ICC's role was later expanded to include jurisdiction over the motor carriers and drivers involved in interstate commerce of all kinds, except for air traffic. In this industry, the ICC controlled permits, approved truck routes, and settled tariff rates.

Kew Gardens Parkway in New York: 1955
(Photo courtesy of Library of Congress: Prints and Photographs Division)

Jack recognized the business potential in the regulatory side of trucking. Understanding that the small trucker in particular had no idea how to deal with these government requirements, Jack decided this was an area where his expertise would be most helpful.

Dealing with the mass of permits needed to carry a product from state to state was, and still is, overwhelming — particularly for truckers with independent streaks. The industry itself was also fiercely competitive and regulated, prompting a need for help in understanding how freight rates varied with the loads they carried.

With a wife and three kids, it took guts for 35-year-old Jack to quit his job at Kampo to begin a new enterprise, J. J. Keller & Associates, as a single office in the 100 block of West Wisconsin Avenue in Neenah. Originally, he worked out of only 1,000 square feet of space within a real estate operation.

"Ethel was my administrative assistant at the time. She answered calls at home, as service was 24 hours, seven days a week," he said.

It was said that Jack started with just a "desk and a phone," but he also had an adding machine which he shipped back from Italy during World War II. He'd found the machine in a blown-out building — such were his spoils of war.

At the time, he had $1,600 to his name, primarily from a $1,200 bonus he'd earned from Kampo. "Realizing that my opportunities were somewhat limited with $1,600, I met with First National Bank President Russ Ward, who was also a friend," he recalled. "He gave me a business loan for $10,000, which set our operation out to tackle the world."

Many years later, in 1991, when Ward attended the grand opening of the company's current corporate offices, he told those in attendance that the $10,000 business loan made to Jack in 1953 was "the best and most productive loan" he'd handled in his 40-year banking career.

Jack opened his office on November 1, 1953 at a time when the nation loved Lucy and liked Ike. Back then, a gallon of milk was just 94 cents, a loaf of bread 16 cents, and a gallon of gas — something important to truckers even if they used diesel — was just 22 cents. In setting out on his business, Jack could have identified with Frankie Laine's hit song of the day, "I Believe."

President Dwight D. Eisenhower

Jack in his first downtown Neenah office: 1953

> *"Ethel was my administrative assistant at the time. She answered calls at home, as service was 24 hours, seven days a week."*

What Jack *did* believe in was that the focus for his new business was very much needed in 1953 and beyond:

- Transportation services within Wisconsin and the nation.

- Insurance services principally to parties involved with transportation, motor vehicle, liability, cargo, and property coverages.

- Warehousing services offering incidental storage as needed for cargo, equipment, and property.

The need for transportation, insurance, and warehousing evolved as motor carriers capitalized on the opportunity to transport goods out of their local areas. "Up to this time, even if carriers could secure the necessary permits, intermediate and long haul transport was virtually impossible as insurance was unavailable," he said.

As far as warehousing, Keller began acquiring old industrial buildings and managed these properties on a percentage lease basis, which didn't require any capital investments on the company's part.

"Over a period of years, we secured over one million square feet of space," Jack said.

The company's reputation grew so large that at one point, Chicago Mayor Richard Daley even contacted Keller about handling the enormous Navy Pier operation in offshore Chicago. Founded in 1909 as a shipping and recreational facility, Navy Pier was in serious decline when the powerful Chicago mayor called Jack.

Navy Pier in Chicago
(Chicago Daily News negatives collection, DN-0066201.
Courtesy of the Chicago Historical Society.)

"I met with Mayor Daley in Chicago to tour the facility, but then gently stepped away from the project," Jack said, "although it was heartening to be considered."

Beyond the basic services, Jack also established a commerce practice called J. J. Keller Commerce Practice to handle license and permit work for motor transportation on an interstate basis.

Moving to 145 West Wisconsin Avenue

Six months after opening his office, Jack and his secretary moved down the street to an office at 145 West Wisconsin Avenue, now called Keller Plaza and home to Zacateca's Mexican Restaurant in downtown Neenah. It was in a building that traces its roots to the 19th century when it was built as a bank and later used as a general store.

Jack quickly had clients calling with a variety of inquiries, including which permits they needed to travel from state to state, tariff rates in different states, and the best truck routes. Jack researched an issue, charging by the hour for his efforts.

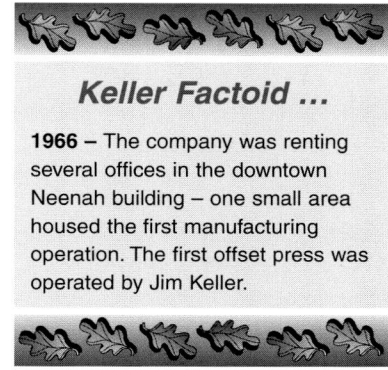

Keller Factoid …

1966 – The company was renting several offices in the downtown Neenah building – one small area housed the first manufacturing operation. The first offset press was operated by Jim Keller.

Truckers then needed to have an ICC permit to haul freight, depending on the truck's classification and the states through which it would travel. "If truckers hauled household goods in the Fox Valley and wanted to go to Chicago and Milwaukee, I would get them an intra-state permit through the ICC. I would tell them the nuances and the costs of trucking permits. Later on, when they had to go to St. Louis, I would get them permits to haul into Missouri. Every state had its own regulations."

The way freight was classified affected shipping costs tremendously — something that would have a great impact on the profitability of a run. "If you make fence posts in Wisconsin and want to ship them four states away, you have to figure out the classification on the posts. Are they painted or stained? Is the fence post hard wood or soft wood? How is the fence post packaged?" Jack asked. "You need an expert to classify the freight so it can go at the lowest rate. You need to have knowledge of everything from ladies underwear to elephants."

Jack's vision was always about providing service, the best possible service to his prospective clients. "The success of the company was based on the concept that there was a need. I did not know to what extent the need would take us; but I knew if we established a varied regulatory service and product line, learned our subject well, analyzed our market well, and presented it properly, we could be reasonably successful," Jack later said in a 1994 interview.

As truckers recognized the expertise that Keller offered, associates were added and more office space was needed. The building at 145 West Wisconsin Avenue, originally divided into retail and professional office space for about 10 tenants, was taken over bit by bit by the company. As businesses left, Jack's growing company acquired their spaces, making building improvements to meet the company's needs. When one of the tenants, a beauty parlor dubbed "the purple palace," left and Keller expanded into its space, the purple shag carpet remained and the smell of perfume wafted in the air for months.

Eventually, when Keller filled half the space, Jack bought the entire building for $86,000 in cash. Avery Sherry, head of the Sherry Corporation which owned the building, gave Jack several thousand dollars in credits for the improvements he had made. Sherry, who had become a friend, said he'd never had a tenant who had made so many improvements in a building.

The year was 1965, and J. J. Keller & Associates, Inc. had 15 associates.

The Wisconsin Avenue office building in Neenah, where J. J. Keller & Associates, Inc. would later occupy the entire space.

The Move into Publishing

One of the major turning points in the company and a reason even more space was needed, according to Ethel, was in 1965 when Jack came home and told her he had better keep the research he'd been compiling because another trucker might come along with the same problem. Among the early projects were studies on truck taxes, including fuel tax reporting. "He thought if someone was willing to pay $5,000 for a study, why not take that study and make it available to a lot of people for $100 or $200. That's the concept of publishing. He'd get the same request five or 10 times and thought if one guy needs it, maybe hundreds need it," Bob recalls.

That was not outlandish thinking by any means. About 40 percent of the business was based on commerce practice activities. "From day one, our business operated on a national scale which created obvious problems, but at the same time gave us national prominence over all," Jack said.

Deciding there was more money to be made in the sale of many publications than in consulting for one client at a time, Jack created his first technical product, the *Exempt Commodities Guide*, and then a four-page informational pamphlet called the *Transportation Journal & Exchange Bulletin*.

The next product, the *Driver's Daily Log Book*, was created after a client who owned a small truck line in Dixon, Illinois asked Jack to critique a competitor's logbook. "I looked at it and saw it contained more information than was required by the federal government, which only wanted records of the number of hours worked and mileage," he said. "It hit me that we could produce a logbook with an addendum of information that would help the truck line owner run his business. The next week I called my staff together with this idea."

Together, the concept of a five-in-one logbook was created to include a grid to log hours of service, mileage, shipments on truck, shipments unloaded, and the driver's inspection of the vehicle. From that single product, which was extremely successful, have come dozens of logbooks. "Now we are the largest logbook publisher in North America," Jack said.

TRANSPORTATION JOURNAL & Exchange Bulletin

JULY 1963   VOLUME I   NUMBER I   NEENAH, WIS.

You are now reading the initial issue of what we believe is an important contribution to the transportation field in Wisconsin and the Midwest. This Journal, along with its companion, "Exchange Bulletin", will endeavor to serve the distributive and transportation industries, both carriers and shippers, in many ways; a few as follows:

BACKGROUND DATA

To provide the industries of Wisconsin an informative service concerning pertinent information surrounding both news and regulation. This material will be presented in a true manner, and where editorialization is used, such efforts will be clearly indicated, and if possible a basis of reasoning for such opinions.

It is our sincere opinion that Wisconsin industry is not receiving adequate information regarding pertinent items that affect their operations. In many cases to a large degree.

TYPES OF BUSINESS SERVED

Much effort will be expended in adequately informing the specialty carriers as to the cause and effect of the current traffic and regulatory trends. It is our opinion that certain elements of the carrier field are reasonably well informed. But the following types of carriage could well use additional guide posts: Private Carriers, Contract Carriers, Regular Route Common Carriers, Leasing Companies, Authorized Rental Companies, Specialty Haulers and Commercial and Industrial Service Groups.

GEOGRAPHICAL SCOPE OF COVERAGE

It is our definite intention to concentrate on immediate problems in the following categories: Local, State, Territorial, National and International.

RESEARCH FACILITIES AVAILABLE

It is further our intention to offer the readership the benefit of research facilities. This will be advisory to some extent. However, no more than now offered through many other types of professional or specialty groups. It is definitely not the intention of this periodical to market "professional services", as such.

The *Driver's Daily Log* was first introduced in the 1960s.

Beyond the logbooks, the next significant publication was the *Trucking Permit Guide* in the late 1960s, which provided state-by-state rules of the road, including permits needed for hauling different products in different states. Like other early Keller products, it was sold before it was fully developed.

"The guide was divided by states. We sent a few states at a time, then a few more states, and a few more states," Jim said. "That actually saved us money."

Keller's advertisements about the benefits of products yet to be produced were highly successful — something that got them into difficulties at times. "When in trouble, we never lied," Bob said. "People respected the truth. We were honorable."

There were occasional complaints about quality, such as logbook covers not matching. "We bought scrap paper and sometimes shipped mixed covers," Bob said.

"In printing, we did the impossible and never turned back," Jim said. "We started from nothing. We use the same concept now."

The *Exempt Commodities Guide* was later revised and the title was changed to the *National Backhaul Guide.* This publication was particularly important because it provided information on what products a trucker could legally haul home on a return journey so the truck wouldn't be empty.

At the heart of these publications was a commitment to accuracy and thoroughness. "You have to be knowledgeable. You can't guess," Jack said. "Half the people who get into this business are not properly trained. I would win many cases as an ICC practitioner because lawyers didn't know traffic and I did. Local lawyers would come in who didn't even know how to spell 'traffic.'"

In the beginning, these publications were little more than typed and mimeographed using tabletop duplicators and AB Dick 360s, technology that was no different than what a teacher might use to produce worksheets in an elementary school. In fact,

AB Dick 360 Printing Press

Bob, now company president, first ran those machines, working after school in the early 1960s. In 1966, the company purchased its first offset press.

When a friend who owned Shiocton Press died, his widow offered their company's printing equipment to Jack, who snapped it up. At that point in the late 1960s, his son Jim was searching for his role in the family business. He enrolled in the Madison Area Technical College's printing program, commuting daily at four-thirty in the morning and returning to Neenah at four-thirty in the afternoon. He then worked until midnight in the pressroom with one other pressman.

Keller Factoid …

Late 1960s – To get paper rolls up to the printing area on the second floor, the company installed a hay elevator (purchased for $400) outside the back of the downtown Neenah building. Thousands of printed pages were taken down the hay elevator, loaded into a van, and transported across the street where the bindery had been set up (now occupied by Caliban's restaurant).

"Dad would say he bought the presses to give me something to do to get me off his back," Jim said, adding, "It was pretty true. We had tried to get into printing with old mimeograph equipment, the kind we had in high school."

Bob's graduation picture: 1965

Jim's graduation picture: 1966

Jim described his dad's first publications as "gospel-like sermons given to the trucking industry, expounding on government rules and regulations."

It didn't take much time for the second floor of the West Wisconsin Avenue building to become a hive of printing activity. Dozens to hundreds of boxes of paper a day, each weighing 30 to 100 pounds, had to be carried up a flight of stairs to the second floor printing press. Then the printed product had to be carried back down those steps to be shipped out to customers. It was backbreaking work.

Veteran Keller associates and brothers Roger and Roy Erdmann

Roy Erdmann, a 33-year veteran press operator with the company, remembered carrying 40-pound boxes of newsprint up those steps. "Sometimes the boxes went tumbling," he said, adding, "We had to haul the paper up those steps to a small room to store all the raw materials. There were a lot of steps."

As Jim remembered, "We had no idea how we would get any productivity out of this."

Then one day, as Jack and Ethel sat in a restaurant in Winneconne, Wisconsin, Jack observed an elevator at work outside a local feed mill moving hay up into a storage facility.

"I thought, 'By God, here's an idea. I could move the paper with an elevator,'" he said.

J. J. Keller & Associates, Inc. purchased a used hay elevator for $400 from Wentzel Ford, an automobile and farm implement dealer in Winneconne.

An old hay elevator similar to the one used by the company

"It was the best $400 we ever spent," Jim said. "We put a reverse on it and put it on a truck in the back alley." They loaded paper into the building with the hay elevator, delivering it through an opening created in a conference room turned into a mini-warehouse. Later, they tore the building open again to move in a paper cutter for the printing operation.

Not all were happy with the Keller industrial revolution, however, especially neighboring downtown retailers. "When it got wet, the elevator squealed and echoed. "We would get complaint calls, 'Can you please do that in non-retail hours?' It was driving them crazy," Jim recalled. "We would unload in early morning and late afternoon to keep the noise level down during retail hours."

As a result, there were major encouragements, if not demands, that Keller at least relocate its printing business from the downtown area. City of Neenah officials especially encouraged the company to relocate as they wanted the land behind the Keller building for a much-needed retail parking lot.

"The city didn't want us and our plant in an area planned for retail," Bob said.

It was getting crowded downtown and the building really wasn't meant for heavy manufacturing work. The 22,000-square-foot downtown building housed the four printing presses on the second floor and other duplicators on the first floor, plus accounting, bindery, editorial, marketing, and services departments — as well as a library of research materials organized and nurtured by Ethel Keller.

Keller Factoid …

1970 –
- Keller employed 20 associates, including staff in the accounting, bindery, editorial, services, and sales departments.
- The company occupied the entire second floor and part of the first floor at 145 West Wisconsin Avenue in downtown Neenah.
- The printing area had two tabletop duplicators and two AB Dick 360 presses.
- Two large mailbags from the first-ever mail campaign were picked up at the Neenah Post Office.

Clearly, the printing presses and related equipment stressed the facilities. And paper, being a very heavy product, was an added burden on the building's structure. Keller also was renting the building across the street to house its paper cutter and as a storage facility.

Needing more production facilities to support the operation and with the city and retail neighbors unhappy with the downtown operation, the company purchased 35 acres of land west of Neenah in the town of Vinland. Construction of the plant began in 1970 and was completed in 1971.

After all the printing equipment moved out, legend has it that the second floor of the building on West Wisconsin Avenue rose by several inches.

Associates from the executive group, marketing, sales, human resources, editorial, product development, and the research and technical library stayed at the downtown office. About 20 years later, the remaining associates moved out to the plant. The office would later be sold to the Future Neenah Development Corporation in May 1992.

Ethel's Library

It wasn't long after Jack told Ethel he'd better start keeping his research materials that he accumulated 30 feet of shelves crammed with books,

> **With a small amount of professional help and a Dewey Decimal System pamphlet, Ethel cataloged all the materials and created a card catalog so associates could easily locate items. Keller's research library was born.**

The first library established by Ethel at the downtown Neenah location

documents, and manuscripts. While there was some semblance of order, it was not exactly a perfect system. That's when Ethel's long-time appreciation of the public library came to fruition.

Taking charge of the "collection," she was determined to organize the materials and establish a research library. Knowing what she wanted to accomplish, but not quite how to go about it, she sought advice from staff at the Neenah Public Library. With a small amount of professional help and a Dewey Decimal System pamphlet, Ethel cataloged all the materials and created a card catalog so associates could easily locate items. Keller's research library was born.

Thanks to Ethel's foresight and determination, those 30 feet of shelves have grown into 2,100 square feet of shelves housing over 9,000 books and audiovisual materials and more than 900 periodical titles. And today, Ethel's card catalog has evolved into an electronic database that makes all items in the collection easily available to every associate.

Dead Animal Room and Other Memories

No discussion of life at Keller can go on without describing the dead animal room (DAR) — of all things, a meeting room at the downtown Neenah office. The walls held dozens of animal trophies, game and fish, including a giant hammerhead shark. As one associate said, "It looked like a sporting goods store."

Jim Keller, a licensed charter captain for 20 years, entertained customers by taking them fishing, doing business as they cast their lines. He caught many of the fish and even shot a few of the animals hanging on those boardroom walls, and prefers to this day to call it the Wisconsin Room even if the associates dubbed it the DAR. Whatever its name, the room was legendary in the company and community.

Jim said the room was meant to give a feeling of Wisconsin's outdoor opportunities to guests. "We would show out-of-state customers what Wisconsin had to offer. People had never seen a wolf or wolverine. We'd show them the perch and walleye you could catch on the Great Lakes. It was unique. It was like a museum."

Todd Lueke, who has worked in the printing area for 23 years in the Town of Vinland plant, remembers the first time he went downtown for his annual review. "I had never even been in the building before. Then I came into the boardroom and saw all these animals and fish on the walls and thought that I might get embalmed — that I was in trouble. I was shocked at that time when I saw the room."

"When people thought of Keller then, it was the DAR that they remembered most," Greg Murray fondly recalled during an interview for this book just a few months before his battle with cancer ended.

Greg Murray with Lila Stenner at her retirement party: 1993

Greg who had worked in the bindery department for 30 years, said the reputation of the room was great in the community, but most people had not even seen it. "A lot of people didn't think the DAR existed. They thought it was a joke."

While most of the stuffed animals are now in storage, there are some remnants of what that room used to be like in Jim's current office. "Now there are 40 fish (on plaques) in my office. It's the new dead animal room," he said.

During the years that Jim was catching all those fish, Keller associates would on occasion find remnants of fish that had been cleaned in the back sinks of the office. "We'd know if Jim had a good weekend or not if we came in on Monday and found cored-out innards of fish in the sink and on office files," said Jan Reh Hamblin, a 28-year sales associate.

Kevin Van Dyn Hoven, who has been in sales since 1978, found fish scales in yet another place. "You'd come in and make coffee first thing in the morning and find scales on the pots."

Jack himself could often be found at the office wearing a fishing hat and a colorful guayabera shirt, the kind of short-sleeved sport shirt commonly worn in South American countries. "He always looked like a man from Panama Beach with his fishing hat on," recalled product editor Pat Laux.

Roy Erdmann remembered long days during his early years with the company. "Twelve hours was nothing. You just came in and got things done. At that time, we assembled books by hand, including the *Trucking Permit Guide* and the *Exempt Commodities Guide*."

Pat Laux recalled the informality of early sales. "In those days, we'd sell a book before all of it was done. "We'd write a couple state sections and send

Pictured clockwise from left at a 1986 Board of Directors meeting in the dead animal room at the downtown Neenah offices are: Ethel Keller, Mary Murvine, Ron Phillips, Jack Keller, Frank "Jack" Pelisek, Jim Keller, and Bob Keller.

them out before all of the sections were finished. Our customers would add them to a binder chapter by chapter."

Initially, Pat worked for Harold Nelson, who had been employed by CW Transport as a dispatcher before joining Keller. When CW Transport moved to Wisconsin Rapids, he didn't want to move with it. Instead Harold, who had been working part-time as a Keller editor, became a full-time associate. "He got to be 'not too bad an editor.' He had never done anything before like proofreading, but he got to be pretty good through on-the-job training," Laux said.

Harold Nelson

Two things were most memorable about Harold Nelson. The first was his vocabulary. "He was a very nice man, but every other word was a swear word," Pat said with a smile. "Harold couldn't talk if he couldn't swear."

The other memory of Harold related to how he died. A man whose devotion to duty and to the Kellers was unlimited, he literally died on the job at a table in the back of the editorial department. "He was helping somebody proofread," Pat recalled. "He keeled over on April Fool's Day. All along Harold said he wanted to die at his desk. He practically did."

Pat Laux at her desk: 1987

Among Pat's other memories are sitting upstairs at the downtown Neenah office in a section of the building that housed both the editorial department and library. "We were just down the hall from the conference room. The executives would be hollering at each other. We'd keep working and right next door they'd be yelling," she said.

Back then, what associates most enjoyed about working for J. J. Keller & Associates, Inc. were the relationships they formed with each other. "We liked who we worked with," Jan Reh Hamblin reflects. And, "we knew just about everyone we worked with," Todd Lueke recalls.

In the early days, they were all members of a tight group of associates. "There were 50 associates when I joined the company and now we have about 950. We've grown a bunch," Pat said. "It's been very interesting in all sorts of areas."

The Space to Grow

With more space, the publishing end of the business really took off. The product line grew from 100 items in 1970 to more than 4,000 today. The staff grew from two associates in 1953, to 20 in 1970, 550 in 1990, and nearly 950 today.

The way the publications look has also come a long way from the days when printed products were merely typed and mimeographed. "Our first products were pretty ugly and poorly designed," Jim said.

"The products looked so bad, a toad looked better," Bob agreed. At one point, the company had an eight-page catalog that didn't change for 11 years. All they would do was insert a flyer from time to time with updated price information or featured items.

"Our first publishing tool was a Selectric typewriter with a little ball. Every page looked the same. That was our typesetting. We couldn't afford to go to a typesetter because of the cost per page," Jim said.

Today, Keller has its own in-house advertising agency to market its products. There are graphic artists and designers on staff to make products more appealing and easy to read and use.

"Now it's packaging and how you deliver the product. You need to put it in a nice book format or binder or CD case. Today, our line has a new millenium look to it," Jim said.

The town of Vinland operation kept expanding to meet the growing workforce and production. In 1970 the original 40,000 square-foot facility was built. Additions included 22,000 square-feet in 1977, 38,750 square-feet in 1979, 88,125 square-feet in 1981, 102,500 square-feet in 1985, and 77,500 square-feet in 1988. The North Park office in 1991 added 120,000 square-feet of space.

The first "Circle-K" sign at the Vinland Complex

"North Park turned out to be one of the finest office facilities in Wisconsin," Jack said. "All of the uptown Neenah staff and equipment were moved to the North Park and Vinland facilities which made for a very efficient operation."

Jack could have moved his company to another state at any time, but chose to stay in Wisconsin, and Neenah in particular. "I was offered residence in Indiana, Georgia, California, and several other states," he said in 1994. "And every time these offers came in, I had more reasons for staying than going." He appreciated Wisconsin's vocational educational system, the work ethic of the people, the ready paper supply in the Fox River Valley, and the state's industrial base and railroad access.

> **Remember when . . .**
>
> ... the sales department was housed in "the box." Some temporary walls were erected in the Vinland warehouse, and that was home for the sales department until we moved into the addition to the north side of the Vinland building which is now tax and safety services.
>
> ... smoking was allowed inside the buildings during work hours. In sales when someone had a baby and cigars were handed out, we would all light them up at the same time. The smoke became pretty thick.
>
> – **Harry Long**
> **Sales**

One of the hallmarks of the company's facilities throughout its history is cleanliness. "Our office is tidy, our shops are tidy, and our warehouse is tidy," Jack once said. "I believe the back of our operation should look as good as the front."

Jack sees a link between a tidy operation and an ethical business practice. "I think if we are professing to be a regulatory advisor, we have to be moral. We have to have character. We have to be honest and we should practice what we preach," he said in that 1994 interview. "We'll work for people who are ethical, but we won't work for anyone who's unethical or dishonest."

Bob is convinced the company's growth would have stalled at $40 million in sales a year without the North Park structure. With this structure, he anticipates the company will soon grow to $250 million in sales — a quarter of a billion dollars — within a decade.

North Park was built in 1991, adding 120,000 square-feet to the facility.

"This building gave us an identity. It gave the people who work here a purpose," Bob said. "We work together more smoothly."

It also gave the company an ability to recruit associates from around the country. "We couldn't have recruited the top people that we have unless we looked good," Jim said. "When we moved out here, our associates said, 'Look at this prominent company.' They were proud to show their families where they work."

Chapter 4

The Boys Enter the Picture

For the children of Jack and Ethel Keller, turning age 12 was a milestone. It was when each of their sons, Bob, Jim, and Tom, were expected to become involved in the business by working after school and during their summers — helping out as best they could. Mostly, their work involved light maintenance, such as mowing the lawn or cleaning the floors. The idea, of course, was to make them a part of the business and to learn to be responsible.

Bob Keller

Jim Keller

Keller Factoid ...

1971 –
- Sales totaled under $500,000.
- Keller opened its new 40,000 square-foot printing facility on Highway 45 in the town of Vinland.

1972 –
- Keller employed 50 associates.
- The company added a health insurance benefit program for associates.

1973 –
- The shipping and warehousing department was staffed by a total of four associates.
- The first edition of the new *Metric Guide* was published.

Bob and Jim would grow into leadership roles with the company. Tom attended college and served in the military prior to working in several areas of the company including the research library. Due to an extended illness, he was placed on permanent disability.

"Dad needed somebody to clean the floors. That's when I got involved. I was indentured. He grabbed me by the throat and told me I was worthless and gave me a mop and bucket," Bob lightheartedly recalled.

"The problem was we were worthless," Jim added, meaning the young boys wanted to help but were limited in their skills at that age.

One day Jack added another chore for Bob, telling him to organize thousands of index cards containing information about Wisconsin truckers and prospective Keller customers. How he was to organize this material was "Bob's problem."

Later, the boys were put to work sorting through tariff fees that the states charged for hauling goods on their roadways. This data was all on loose pieces of paper. After spending hours on this particular project, Bob was nearly halfway finished when Jack wanted something else done with the information.

Working for the company back then did not provide big money. Bob remembers getting paid something like 50 cents an hour. "Dad said he couldn't afford 70 cents," Bob recalled.

Jim still has a paycheck stub from 1969 when he began working full-time. It shows him making a whopping $180 for 72 hours of work — $2.50 an hour.

Bob struggled when he first went to high school, having

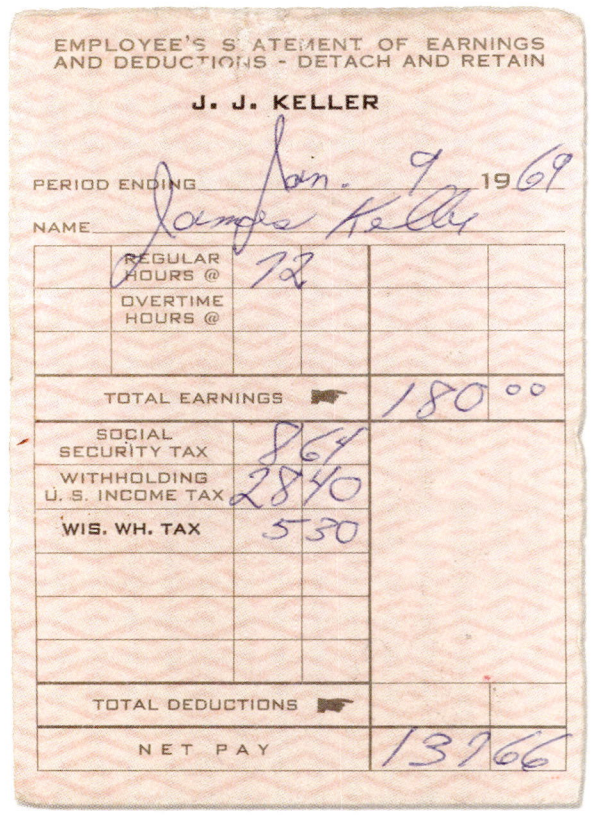

Jim's first paystub: 1969

Jim with Dave Ellis inspecting a catalog cover proof: mid-1980s

gone to a country school for elementary grades where older students primarily tutored the younger ones. "I got to high school and I couldn't read. I had a blank look, like a deer caught in the headlights. An English teacher noticed and got me help."

With work and perseverance, Bob made great progress. "I could read in a short period of time, then I taught myself how to speed-read," he recalled. In fact, Bob became so comfortable with the written word that he would quickly read books at the end of a college semester, just before the exams. He could then visualize or recall what he needed when it came time for the test. "Several days later I'd forget it all," he said.

Jim's strength was numbers. "He could look at a page of numbers and see the one that was wrong," Bob said.

As they became adults, the roles Bob and Jim were to fulfill in the company were further defined.

Bob, who earned a degree from the University of Wisconsin-Oshkosh in economics, held a number of positions within the company during the early years, including advertising and marketing manager. He was appointed senior vice president in May 1973, executive vice president in 1974, and took on the additional responsibilities as chief operating officer in 1977. He was appointed president in 1983, and since 1988 has served as president and chief executive officer.

Jim, who earned a graphic arts degree from the Madison Area Technical College, also held a number of positions in the company during the early years, including manager of the graphics and production division, corporate secretary, and controller. In 1973, he became vice president of production with a promotion to vice president of operations in 1974. Jim then became senior vice president in 1977. He was appointed executive vice president in 1983, and since 1987 has served as executive vice president and chief operating officer.

Working side-by-side with their dad, Bob and Jim certainly appreciated the magnitude of ideas that came out of his head. "He had great ideas. But he was always starting stuff and never quite finishing anything," Bob said. "Dad had hundreds of ideas in a week. We couldn't even process them all."

"He was a typical ideas guy. We watched so many ideas come and go and so many potential products fall away," Jim added.

During the 1960s and 1970s as they came into adulthood and grew in their leadership roles with the company, Bob and Jim always worked six days a week.

"On the weekends, dad dictated for hours and hours and hours on an old dictation machine with wax rolls. The secretaries took all of the next

A sales meeting at the downtown Neenah offices: early 1970s

week to transcribe the memos from dad. Some days we'd get quarter-inch thick memos," Bob recalled.

Some of those memos would have 10 to 20 concepts running through them, using Jack's own characteristic style, which included some words of his own making and a uniquely personal punctuation style.

"Dad had dreams to grow the company business big enough for the family," Bob said, adding, "He didn't care what we did as long as we were good at it."

While Jack was happy to have his sons, and later grandchildren, join him in the business, he felt the wives shouldn't be a part of it. "I have enough trouble dealing with you kids," he used to say.

Added Jim, "Papa Bear had two cubs floundering around trying to make a living."

Keller Family Life

The women who married Bob and Jim Keller really married the business. Long hours, particularly during the first decades of their marriages, were the norm for their husbands. The hours may be somewhat shorter today, but these women understand the commitment it takes to keep a business successful — especially one that now supports not only theirs, but 950 families.

Jim met his wife Rosanne in high school, but it was at the wedding of her cousin, Greg Drews, who works at Keller, that they met each other again. Jim and Rosanne began dating and were married on October 9, 1976.

Rosanne remembers the early years of their marriage when everyone at Keller knew each other and their spouses so well they went to each other's weddings and special events. As Jim's wife, she thought it was important to be involved in these events and to know all of the associates and their families by name, a role that has become more difficult as the company has grown.

"One of the things I realized early on is that Jim lives, eats, and breathes his work,"

Jim and Rosanne's wedding photo: 1976

she said. "He tries to leave it at the office as much as possible when he comes home, getting involved in fishing, and doing things with the family."

"And more fishing," Jim added.

So important is the sport, in fact, that Rosanne found herself going fishing on their honeymoon, a three-week, leisurely trip out west. She should have realized what her life would be like when they made a dash back from Jackson Hole, Wyoming to Eagle River, Wisconsin just to see what was biting there. What they discovered was water so cold that the propeller on their boat froze.

"Do I love to fish?" she asked. "I love him. If you love him, you fish."

Has life changed for her in more recent years? "I don't know that the hours have changed. Jim is so committed to the business," Rosanne said. "Last night, he called after seven o'clock in the evening and said he was just trying to get out of the office. I don't think there's any separation between the business and the family. That can be good or bad. In fact, a lot of business is done outside of work, on weekends and even holidays. When we get together as an extended family, so much of the business is being discussed, planned, and figured out."

> **Remember when . . .**
>
> *. . . we used to produce six-up log books the old-fashioned way. First we would receive a paste-up from the composition department and photograph it onto photo mechanical transfer (PMT) material through a horizontal camera. After several time-consuming steps, we would expose the film to a metal plate, and bring it to a wash station where we would scrub off the unexposed material using a very strong chemical, wash with water and then cover the plate with a gum arabic to prevent oxidation. Now it's ready for press. Let's just say we've come a long way baby!*
>
> — **Randy Rowe**
> **EPS Administration**

When they were 14, Bob and Lynne met each other on the school bus, although Bob had first seen and admired Lynne from a distance one day when he saw her horseback riding. They were high school sweethearts who continued dating while Bob was in college.

With Bob running the mimeograph machine after school, their dates were unconventional, often starting at 10 o'clock in the evening. "My dad would get irritated. He said that was when you were supposed to come home, not leave," Lynne recalled.

Lynne did understand the lifestyle of a family business. Her father, the late John Cumings, owned an electrical contracting business. "I was brought up in a family business. A family business lifestyle was normal for me," she said. Today, Lynne has her own business managing rental properties.

Lynne recalls during their dating years that Ethel would answer the phone for the company at home while Jack was on the road. In those days before call waiting and voice mail, all personal calls had to be kept to 10 minutes so clients would not be missed. There wasn't much time to court over the phone.

"In the early years after our marriage in 1968, I worked sun-up to six o'clock in the evening," Bob recalled. "I worked seven days a week for 15 years and six days a week for another 10 to 15 years."

Family suffered by those hours. "It haunts me to this day," Bob said. "It was really hard on my wife. She often called the business my mistress. There was a feeling of overburden."

Bob and Lynne's wedding photo: 1968

Bob and Lynne Keller

Jim and Rosanne Keller

Chapter 5

The Third Generation

For the third generation of Kellers, growing up "Keller" was both easy and hard. All the Keller grandchildren have financial security; but also, much is expected of them, whether they choose to work for the company or take an entirely different direction in their lives.

Bob and Lynne have four children: Marne, born in 1969; Rustin, born in 1972; Rachael, born in 1974; and Adam, born in 1978. Jim and Rosanne have two children: Brian, born in 1980, and Angela, born in 1984. Tom does not have children.

A fourth generation has begun as well. Marne and her husband, Alec have two children: Madeleine, born in 1996, and Quinten, born in 2000. Rachael and her husband, Phil have two children: Grace, born in 2000, and Noah, born in 2003. Rustin and his wife, Christina are expecting their first child in summer 2003. And, Brian and his wife, Melissa are expecting their first child in the fall of 2003.

Marne Keller-Krikava
Strategic Planning

In addition to growing up in strong, supportive families, the grandchildren also have financial security, unlike many young people their age. It was about the time when Rosanne was pregnant with Angela that Jack started to distribute shares of company stock to his grandchildren, including the unborn grandchild dubbed "U-B Keller" or "unborn Keller." "I was always my grandfather's little U-B. I was the only stockholder with stock before I was born," she said.

The challenge for Angela during her adolescent years, mostly in middle school, was that her classmates expected her to have and do more for them financially because they assumed she had money. Some assumed she'd pay for things for them. "I did get picked on from time to time," she said. "When we'd drive by the Keller buildings, they'd say, 'Angela, there's your company,' stuff like that."

Rachael and Adam did not have that experience. They came of age at a time when the company was less well-known or at least less visible, because the North Park office was not yet constructed. "Most of my friends couldn't relate to the business," Adam said.

"I felt pretty anonymous in high school," Rachael said. "Then some of my friends started working at the company."

Rustin Keller
Keller Online

The reality is that the Kellers raised very grounded children because they are grounded themselves. Rustin, Bob and Lynne's oldest son, tells the response of a classmate the first time he came to their house. "This is a Keller house?" the friend said. "No offense, but I expected something more."

The Kellers, from Jack on down, are not flashy people. "We did not grow up any differently than anyone else," Rustin said. "We had a small house, a normal house. And, our grandparents' house was just like anyone else's."

When Bob and Lynne's family took road trips, their children were not encouraged to play that classic highway game of finding something that started with each of the letters of the alphabet. Instead, they became unofficial members of the Keller marketing team. "Our kids watched for trailer signs and markings, watching for ones that didn't have the Keller name on them so we could contact them," Lynne said.

In her own travels, Lynne found that the Keller name came in handy when she stopped for a meal at a truck stop in Georgia late one night. "I didn't realize I was out of cash and had not one credit card with me. All I had was a local check from Neenah. I saw a Keller logbook in the back," she said. "I said, 'See, my checks have the same address.' They cashed my check. No questions asked."

The Keller grandchildren also had opportunities for special times with Jack and Ethel, including a trip to Florida each child took when he or she reached age 10. "I loved it," Marne said. "It was without my siblings."

On occasion, she'd take the bus to her grandparents' home after school. After a snack, she'd practice the piano, which her grandmother loved to hear.

Marne with her grandparents and father: 1982

One of the amusing oddities of life as a Keller occurred as a result of Jack's business venture in the soap business years earlier. At that time, he purchased cream rinse and other toiletry products by the case, and the girls did not have a choice of hair products that others their age had. They used leftover cream rinse instead of conditioner, which was a more popular choice for girls their age. "It was not until I was a teenager that the old stock of cream rinse finally ran out," Marne said.

To this day, Bob regrets that he lived and breathed the company, working long hours that left him less time for his family, something that is quite common in a growing family business. Bob credits Lynne with doing a wonderful job with the children when he worked so much. "I didn't realize until later the impact my hours would have on the kids, there's no doubt in my mind," he said.

The children do remember those long hours. "Until I was a teenager, 90 percent of dad's awake time was at work, from six o'clock in the morning to six o'clock in the evening," Rustin said. "He'd get up at four-thirty in the morning and read work-related materials until six and then go into work. He'd come home at six at night, eat, and then be asleep by eight. Though, when I got to be a teenager, he started to loosen up a bit."

Keller Factoid ...

1974 –
- The company added 2,000 square-feet to the downtown Neenah office.
- The "Diamond K" logo was first used and became a registered trademark on March 11, 1975.
- Keller offered a new publication, the *Trucking Safety Guide*.
- The services sales department was formed with two associates.

> **Remember when . . .**
>
> ... in 1995, Keller had only five PCs connected to the Internet. John Breese and I built a mini-Intranet so associates using the walk-up PCs could easily access the same information.
>
> – Bill Kelly
> Keller Online

Marne said the hours were such that she didn't know her father well until she was an adult working at the company. "His life was work. My time with him was from five to six o'clock in the morning. When I was about three, I started drinking coffee with him — with a lot of sugar and cream," she recalled. "When people ask what my fondest childhood memories are, one of them is of Saturday mornings when dad would take me to Kresge's in downtown Neenah for coffee."

One reason for the long hours, Marne believes, is that her father felt the weight of the responsibility for the families who worked at Keller. "He wanted to make sure the people and their families were well-provided for."

Entering the Family Business

According to Bob, none of the children were told they had to go into the family business. But, all were told they needed to continue their education beyond high school. This attitude is similar to what Bob heard from his own father as he and his brothers became adults. "I didn't force my boys to work for me. I let them make up their own minds," Jack said.

As was true for the second generation, the children of Bob and Lynne started working for the company when they turned 12. They were there to learn the work ethic that all parents hope their children embrace. They also wanted them to understand the company business and appreciate what they have.

"They started at the bottom so they would know what this company is about," Lynne said. "We felt if they started at the top, they would not get the needed background or experience."

As young Keller associates, nearly all of their wages were put into savings accounts for college. To help their children learn to handle money, Bob and Lynne put their children on strict budgets, giving them set amounts each month for items such as shoes and clothing. At least one of the children knew how to squeeze his pennies, saving just about everything given to him. "Rustin didn't spend any money on clothes. His shoes were falling off his feet," Lynne recalls.

Marne's first job involved helping her grandmother plan the annual company picnic. "Grandma took me downtown and we'd get everything ready for the summer picnic, including all the little toys for the kids," she recalled. "The highlight for me was after we were done, she'd take me for Chinese food down the street. In our family, we never went out for dinner. With four kids, it would have cost a fortune."

The grandchildren have the opportunity for careers with the company, which three of the six have accepted, much to the pride of their grandfather. "I have no objection if they want to come into the company. That's great," Jack said, "Or they can do something else."

Except for the year between high school and college when Marne was in Denmark as an exchange student, she has worked for the company. She came back from Denmark with an interest in international business. "I just ended up staying," she said.

Brian joined the company full-time in 2000 after he discovered a special interest in computer programming. After graduating from high school, he went to the University of Wisconsin-Oshkosh. During Christmas break, while recovering from surgery for a high school football injury, he found himself tinkering with computers.

Brian Keller
Tax & Safety Services

"I couldn't drive for six weeks. That's when I decided to start my fishing business, Reel Hooked Guide Service. Then I taught myself to build a website and found out I like to do this stuff," he said. "After I finished my first year of college, I went to Fox Valley Technical College, where I earned an associate degree in PC support and web development."

Today, Brian is a programmer for *www.kellerservices.com*, a job that is an electronic version of the graphics work that young Jim Keller did a few decades earlier. Having worked at Keller part-time since he was 16, Brian feels comfortable continuing with the company as an adult. "I've been working here forever and everybody knows me."

"Most people don't think of me as a Keller, to be honest," Brian said. "Part of it is the upbringing from my parents. None of us are any better than anyone else. You show up and work five days a week like everyone else and you work longer if a project needs to get done. Being a Keller doesn't give you an excuse to leave early."

Brian married Melissa Mesich in March 2002. Melissa has been with the company since 1999 and is now a sales training and program specialist.

Brian has enjoyed talking with his grandpa, learning about the development of Keller over the last five decades. "Now with all this business corruption, all the Enrons and WorldComs and everything going on, it's nice to have a family-owned business that is legitimate and has been around for 50 years," Brian said. "Grandpa himself would never do anything unethical. He is probably the most ethical person there is. Grandma is the same way. She is as straight-laced as they come."

Keller Factoid ...

1975 –
- The *Driver's Safety Pocket Book* was added to the product line.
- Profit-Sharing & Retirement Plan benefit program was established for associates with an initial contribution of $15,000.
- Keller signed a contract with NCR for the first computer system.

1976 –
- Keller employed 96 associates.
- Keller offered two snap-out forms. Today there are 56 snap-out forms.
- The first Didde-Glaser two-color, roll-to-roll web press was installed.

Rustin remembers his grandfather asking only once or twice whether he'd join the company, but more questions came from other associates, who frequently would ask, "Are you going to grow up and take over Keller? I'd say, 'No, not really.' At the time, I couldn't envision a future here. I thought I would do something on my own," he said.

The question is a poignant one for Rustin, considering he was about 12-years-old when his father, at age 37, became president of J. J. Keller & Associates, Inc. "I don't think people realize at what cost that comes to the kids of the business owners," he said. "I remember one time my father said that people don't understand the responsibility of making sure all those people and their families are provided for."

That message became clear to Rustin when he was a supervisor for GE Medical in Milwaukee, after graduating with a bachelor's degree in industrial engineering from Marquette University. "From time to time, people would come to my office. One woman told me her husband had left her. Another had cancer. All of these problems go to the boss," he said. "You don't know that until you're a boss."

During his three years at GE Medical, Rustin completed the firm's two-year management training program, which gave him exposure to various roles that are helpful to him now that he is at Keller. He served as production support engineer, production team leader, information systems project leader, and pricing analyst. As a consultant for imaging services with GE, he took a lead role in a team responsible for process redesign, information system implementation, and receivables collections projects for a national diagnostic imaging network group.

Rustin found when he returned to join J. J. Keller & Associates, Inc. in 1999 that few people knew who he was. "When I came here, I expected a lot more grief, but I didn't see it."

Marne feels that as part of the Keller family, they are watched to see if they really deserve to be in leadership roles in the company, and if they are working as hard as others in the company.

Deanna DeVooght, sales planning and promotion manager, joined Keller about the same time as Marne in 1991. "Marne is as hard working as anyone else. In my opinion, the image of the Kellers is they work above and beyond what is expected of them because of the feeling that people are looking to them for leadership."

Regardless of whether anyone is keeping an eye on them to see if they do their share, Marne said her father instilled a strong work ethic in his children, making sure they recognize that being a Keller does not give them special privileges. As an example, when she was younger, she once asked her father to bring home paper and pencils imprinted with the Keller company name. "He said no, that associates would be fired for that."

Taking Different Roads

Bob and Lynne's two younger children, Rachael and Adam, have chosen other career paths, despite working for the company from age 12 like their older siblings. Adam worked on maintenance and property crews, while Rachael worked in fleet operations. They, too, remember no special privileges. Adam, in fact, recalled someone he knew earning more per hour than he did for the same job. Rachael remembered the parent-imposed savings plan that began with her first paycheck.

"I worked 12 hours, got $30, and only kept 10 percent or three dollars," she said. "The rest had to go in my bank account."

Adam Keller

Adam's original plan was to become an architect. He was not far into his studies at the University of Wisconsin-Milwaukee, however, when he realized his design interests were for living quarters for species other than humans. At age 19, he started Cages by Design, a company which his website describes as an "enclosure manufacturer" for exotic animals. How successful can selling custom-designed reptile cages be?

His cages sell from about $200 to $500. With accessories, the average order is $800. His company had a half-million dollars in sales in 2000 and was expecting one million dollars in sales in 2002, mostly through his website *www.cagesbydesign.com*, direct mail, and in-person sales.

While in high school, the first cage he ever built took up a quarter of his bedroom. Other cages, relegated to the basement, took up much more space. "There was a 12-foot by 12-foot cage for my iguana, which was only nine inches long," Adam recalled. "I liked building cages more than anything."

Adam's mother wasn't as fond of the cages — or what was in them — as Adam believed. "His horrible creatures in the basement," Lynne recalled. "He never liked them ... he just liked building the cages," she said.

Adam admits to a streak of independence. "I have always wanted to work for myself," Adam said. "I don't care what I do, I never want to work for someone else. I would rather make $5,000 a year and live in a van down by the river than work for somebody else."

That entrepreneurial spirit clearly is reminiscent of Jack Keller. Adam already suggests that he'll keep designing and selling cages until he is bored with that enterprise. Then he'll find something else, "like grandpa."

In fact, he frequently consulted with Jack during the early days of his business. "I wanted to show grandpa my plans for the business and talk to him about it," Adam said. "We spent a lot of time together."

Keller Factoid ...

1977 –
- The Fox Cities Chamber of Commerce & Industry presented an award to Jack Keller for his efforts in improving the company's facilities.
- Keller provided services to 300 clients.
- A new publication was introduced — the *Hazardous Materials Guide*.
- The company purchased a Didde-Glaser Web-Klect roll collator to use for collating and assembling logbooks and numerous other snap-out forms.
- A new regulation resulted in the development of a new line of Keller products — placards and placard holders.

Like her siblings, Rachael worked for the company every summer. "I never felt there was pressure to work here after college graduation. In fact, I always knew that I wanted to work with kids," she said.

Now a kindergarten teacher at East DePere Elementary School south of Green Bay, she is proud to have completed her education program at Carroll College in Waukesha, Wisconsin in four years instead of the more common five years for an education major. In 1996, she took a long-term substitute position in DePere and then began her teaching career at the second grade level. She soon found her niche to be kindergarten.

Rachael does carry with her the values she learned from the family business. "When I go into a meeting, I want to get things done the most efficient way," she said. "I treat my classroom like a business, looking at my students and their parents as customers."

Rachael Keller-Graebel

Committed to these "customers," she helps children learn values that will help them be successful in life. "If parents come in and ask how their child is doing, I have samples ready, a portfolio, anything that might show them rather than just talking in vague terms. I want something to back me up."

The assets in her classroom — the children — are what excites Rachael. "The kids love going to school. Parents tell me that even when they are sick, their children want to go to school."

After graduating in 2002 from Winneconne High School, Jim and Rosanne's daughter Angela is continuing her education at the Fox Valley Technical College in interior design. She plans to earn a four-year degree after technical college.

Angela worked summers at Keller during high school. "I worked in the tax and safety services department doing a lot of computer work and filing. I was also in the warehouse for part of that time," she said.

Even family members who are not associates have a genuine interest in the company, according to Bob. "They know what's going on. They know what the business is about because they attend stockholders' meetings. They have a sense that the family is involved with something important that their fathers and grandfather developed."

Angela agrees, saying she is proud of what her grandpa and other family members have accomplished. "My grandpa started from a very humble beginning. My grandpa, father, and uncle turned Keller into a major company," she said.

Angela Keller

"I've always gone to stockholders' meetings and different functions. The last three years, I've gone to the American Trucking Associations' convention with my mom and dad. By going to the meetings, I've really gotten to watch my dad be hands-on, and I've been able to learn a lot about the company by listening to people. It's been a really neat learning experience."

Marne Keller-Krikava and husband Alec

Rachael Keller-Graebel and husband Phil

Rustin Keller and wife Christina

Brian Keller and wife Melissa

Chapter 6

Growing Up

By the time the company had incorporated in 1958, J. J. Keller & Associates, Inc. had grown to six associates. The initial incorporation included 5,000 shares of stock with an initial value of $10 a share.

The standard operating procedure for J. J. Keller & Associates, Inc. in the 1960s and 1970s was OPM — "Other People's Money." With little or no capital, they had to use their ingenuity to have the funds to operate.

"We were trained on other people's money," Bob said. "We paid on revolving credit, but wanted other people's money in advance for our products and services."

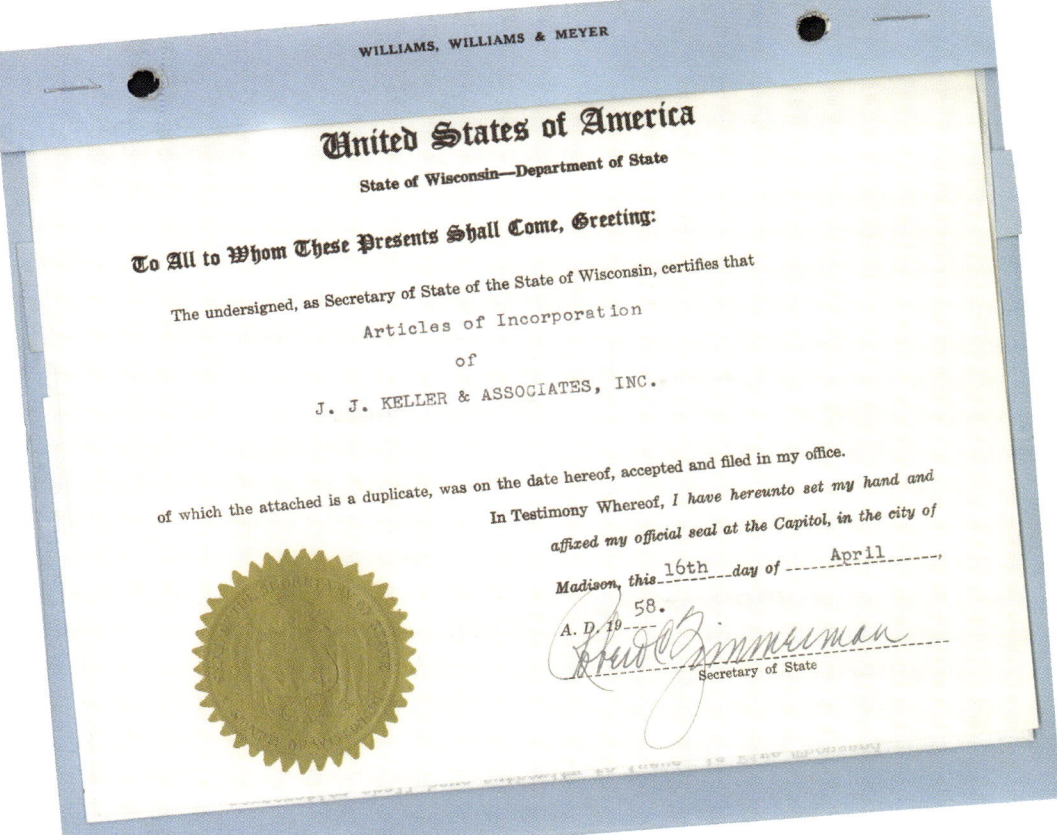

Incorporation papers: 1958

One of the services Keller provided was paying the taxes and permits for truckers. This meant that for an upfront fee, Jack Keller handled the paperwork — holding the funds in an escrow account until the services were performed.

As they began their publishing business, they sold multiple-year subscriptions to their publications, collecting three or more years' worth of update fees up-front before the first update was ever delivered. "Dad was a capitalist without capital," Bob said.

Even a capitalist without capital needs money to begin a new operation, such as publishing. Confident the banks would recognize the value of what the company wanted to do, Jack sought a $25,000 business loan. Today, when banks are eager to lend money and compete for customers, it's hard to imagine how difficult it was to get a business loan for a new concept in those days.

Jack discovered the banks were not eager to lend the money. "The banks said that publishers were located in New York, not Neenah. They turned us down," Jim said. "So dad took Bob and me to the bank and we each borrowed $10,000 in personal money. He grabbed us by the scruff of the neck and had us each sign for $10,000 to be repaid over five years."

In exchange for taking on that debt, the boys were given some stock in the company, making them part owners. "We had to put our money where our mouths were," Jim said.

Keller Factoid ...

1978 –
- Keller employed 175 associates.
- A 22,000 square-foot addition to the Vinland plant was completed.
- The triple flag pole set was erected in front of the plant site, bearing the American flag, Wisconsin State flag, and a Diamond K logo flag.
- A second web press (three-color, roll-to-sheet) was installed in the manufacturing area.

How did J. J. Keller & Associates, Inc. move from OPM to today's debt-free operation? "We learned how to be good money managers and operational planners," said Jim.

One of Bob and Jim's most important roles with the company was taking Keller from a shoot-from-the-hip firm to one with operations based on strategies and planning. "Until about 1985, we operated like most small businesses — by the seat of our pants. Then we got serious about planning and equipment. We realized that when you have hundreds of associates, you better be serious about what you're doing," Bob said.

Planning was needed to take the company from the "pure ideas of Jack Keller" to a structured environment. With so much growth under foot, the challenge was keeping associates who were having difficulty adjusting to this rapidly changing culture.

Jack at the first Vinland construction site: 1971

"Keller was a struggling young company in the '70s and '80s. It was not the kind of company that could offer the same type of pay and benefits as other companies that had been around for years and years," Mark Tremble, senior vice president of sales and marketing, said. "We were always looked upon as an orphan."

Part of the problem was the turnover rate at this very hectic company. The other was that the local people simply did not understand what the company did. It did not manufacture paper or grow food, things that most people understood. Its marketplace was national, however.

Keller survived its many challenges, Mark said, because it's a company based on "intellectual property." It safeguards its products through copyrights.

Community opinions about the company changed dramatically in later years. "Now it is seen as a huge, respected operation," Terry Quirk, senior vice president of publications and products, said.

"Its reputation in the Fox Valley is so minimal compared with its reputation in the United States, Canada, and some foreign countries," Mark said. "People in our industry know this company. You go to a trade show in Las Vegas where there are 50,000 people, and 80 percent know Keller. It's unbelievable. It's because of our expertise and reputation and because we are dedicated to quality, excellence, and community service."

In 1971, after Keller had built its first production facility, sales rose to $500,000. From 1953 to 1973, combined company sales did not even total $1 million in business, but from 1973 to 2000, sales reached $1 billion accumulatively, according to Jim. "The business took off, starting from a lone practitioner who could only make money by charging a fee for his time."

The growth was not without pain, however. With the company sometimes stretched thin in its years of rapid growth, every penny counted — literally. "Everything was traumatic. A one-cent increase in mailing costs was a nightmare," Mark said. "We worked very hard every day to meet the payroll. I just wanted a steady paycheck and insurance. And, through it all, Keller never missed a payday."

A Company of Associates

Back when J. J. Keller & Associates, Inc. was beginning to move beyond a company that was just Jack and Ethel, the "associates" part of the business name was taken very seriously. Those who worked for the company then and now are "associates," not employees or staff, something that reflects Jack's philosophy.

> **Remember when . . .**
>
> ... sales was downtown, and order processing and credit were in the new Highway 45 building. Sales orders were written, put in suitcases, and delivered to the offices at the new location to get processed.
>
> – **Mary Pamer**
> **Publications Credit**

"I've always believed in a team effort. That's why the company emphasizes the "associate principle," where associates share the responsibilities and share the results," Jack commented at the time of the company's 35th anniversary.

Why take that approach? "The first thing you have to realize is that you can't know everything. You always have to respect the intelligence of others," Jack said. "In our company we always do that. You don't see me with my door closed. If anybody wants to talk with me or anyone else, they are free to do so."

Jack developed this philosophy because of his own experience working for companies where he was not considered a part of the team. "Very few companies successfully establish the associate principle because it has to come from the top down. The officers or owners of the company have to accept it, and so do its employees. It has to be mutual."

Terry Quirk came to Keller in 1974 as an editor from Washington, D.C. "I knew about the Keller name. I wrote George McDowell (editorial department supervisor at the time) who got Keller to invite me for an interview."

On the evening he arrived, Terry, who then had long hair and a beard and wore jeans and a tweed jacket, didn't expect to meet the Kellers until the next morning. But taking a hands-on approach to a prospective new associate, Jack and Ethel came to the Valley Inn in Neenah to greet him.

"It was great. Jack and Ethel were very, very cordial. The time flew by," he said. "We sat and talked and drank Dewars scotch until midnight. It was cool to meet the president and his wife, and I can say I was truly impressed. I had a great night."

Terry Quirk: 1974

Ron Phillips: 1977

Ron Phillips, now senior vice president of finance, knew he didn't want to raise a family in Florida, so when his wife's sister moved to Appleton, he and his wife decided to look at the Fox Cities as well. It was Christmas 1976 when he had his first look at Keller.

"It seemed like a nice company and it looked like there was some potential for growth," said Ron, who was hired as controller. Ron has been an associate ever since.

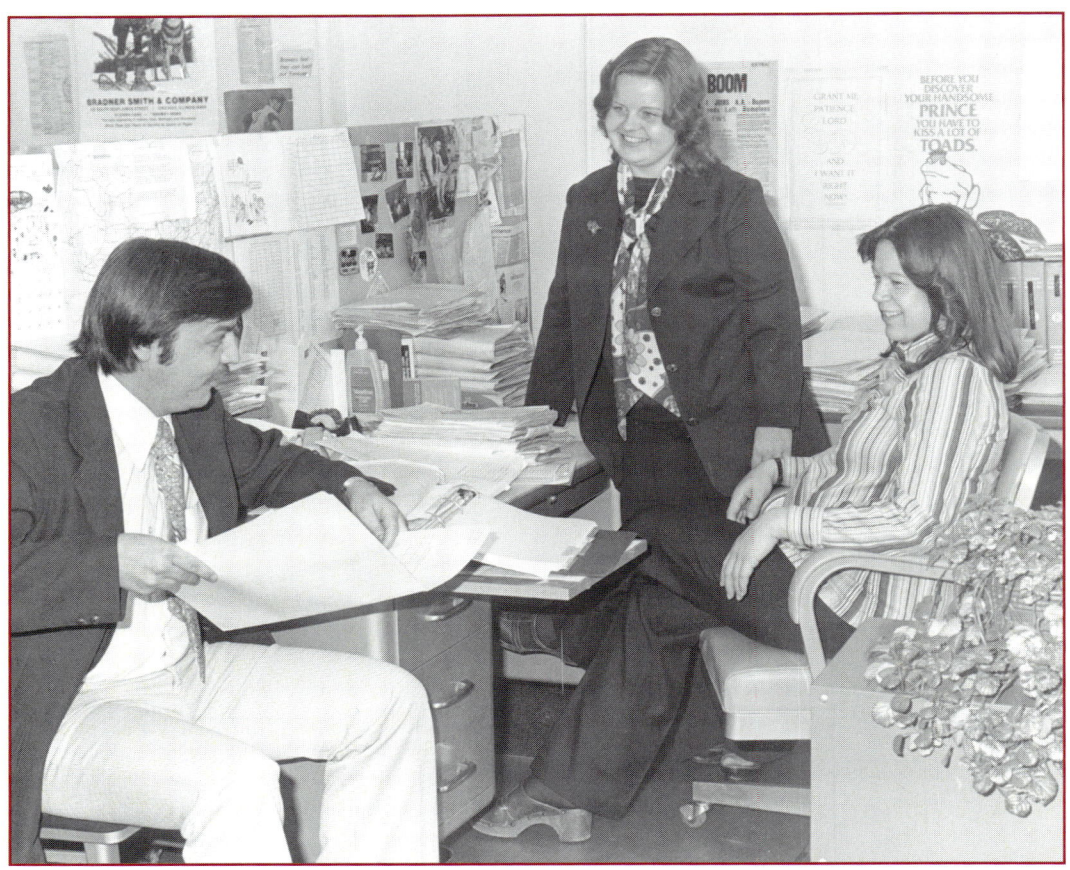
Customer service associates Dave Ellis, Jan Reh Hamblin, and Becky Gatza: 1979

Telephone Sales

At the heart of the company's growth was a commitment to customer service. "We were brutal when it came to customer service and quality. That was our strength. The people were our strength," Bob said.

Even today, Bob never discards a note about a customer call until he is convinced the client's concern is resolved to his or her satisfaction. Even if the call comes on a Saturday to his home, he makes sure the need is resolved.

One reason that J. J. Keller & Associates, Inc. needed more associates was that the company was about to become a pioneer in the new field of telemarketing, something that was partly one of Jack's big ideas, according to Bob. Jack brought in an article about a chemical distributor in Ohio who had a five-lady telephone sales team. He said, "If they can sell chemicals using these 'chickies,' we can do something with this, boys — we can add a couple of chicks ourselves."

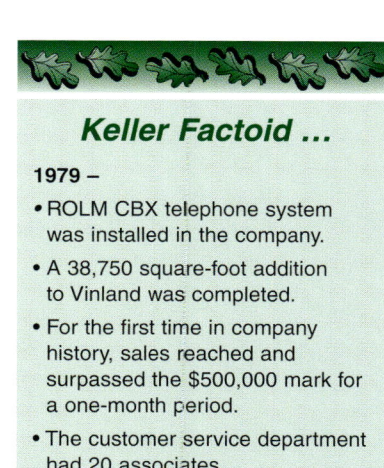

Keller Factoid …

1979 –
- ROLM CBX telephone system was installed in the company.
- A 38,750 square-foot addition to Vinland was completed.
- For the first time in company history, sales reached and surpassed the $500,000 mark for a one-month period.
- The customer service department had 20 associates.
- The first Horizon Club banquet was held, honoring 52 associates.

"Dad had the ability to sniff out these trends," Bob added.

The first hired in this role was Kay Deeg, who added a couple of other "chickies," herself. While it is no longer politically correct to refer to women as chicks or chickies, it was a different time in the 1950s and 1960s.

What was true then and now is that the "truckers loved the women," Bob said. "To this day, our sales force is mostly female on the telephone dealing with predominantly male truckers. Kay Deeg built up quite a successful work team."

Jan Reh Hamblin was an early telemarketer who has been with the company since 1975, and is now corporate special markets sales manager. "I was very young and stupid," she said. "At that time telemarketing was not a term that was out there, but I was able to get on the phone and try to sell some stuff."

These pioneering telemarketers were naïve, with no idea how to sell over the phone. "Nobody told us it would work. We just called and wrote orders," Jan said.

Sales department: 1988

The women on the sales force were bubbly and friendly and able to deal with truckers who could at times be rough in their language and centered on their own needs. These attitudes were a result of the many hours they spent alone on the road. They liked to hear a warm and flattering female voice when they called in with a question or to order a product.

"Truckers were softies for the women on the phone. And this was before telemarketing was even invented," Jim said.

Becky Gatza, who also has been in sales since 1973 and is now senior transport sales manager, said, "We were young. We didn't know any better. There was no plan. We just dove in. You did what you did, and you made up the rules as you went."

Pat Laux, a 31-year veteran and now product editor, said the company had another motivation for becoming inadvertent pioneers in telephone sales. "They wanted the sales people where they could keep an eye on them. They didn't want them running away from the office."

In his 28 years with the company, Mark Tremble saw the transition of a company dominated by men to one with tremendous opportunities for women. He joined the company in 1975, a time when the product line consisted of no more than 25 to 50 products.

"When I was hired, we had a small sales department. There were product sales along with some services sales, like permitting and tax reporting," he said.

Kay Deeg, who had been with the company about six months longer than Mark, trained him to make the move from general sales to telephone sales. She also hired the original team of women who would be so effective in working with the male truckers.

Keller Factoid ...

1980 –

- The safety committee was established to review safety concerns and recommend actions.
- The company had 230 associates, 88 typewriters, and 205 calculators.
- The first word-processing equipment was installed in the downtown offices.
- Construction began on an 88,125 square-foot addition to the Vinland Complex.
- The company showed a 30% increase in product sales and a record of over $6 million in sales.
- A new Didde-Glaser 860 web press was installed, capable of making 35,000 impressions per hour.

Mark Tremble: 1987

It was a stressful job. "The hours were sunrise to sunset," said Mark, who came to the company with a degree in geology and anthropology, along with a teaching certificate.

Getting Promoted

To become senior vice president of sales and marketing and senior vice president of publications and products respectively, Mark Tremble and Terry Quirk had to have their share of promotions over the years. How were these promotions noted?

Literally, by the size of their desktops. With word of a promotion, someone would come in and unscrew the old desktop and attach a new, bigger and supposedly better one.

"In those days, we used to move our own furniture. We had heavy metal desks, old Army desks, and it took four guys to lift one. The more you were promoted, the bigger top you got," Mark recalled.

"One desk top was so large," Terry added, "we called it the aircraft carrier. It didn't even fit into the cubicle. I guess the thinking was that the more important you were, the more paperwork you did. Thus, you needed more desk space."

An early aerial view of Vinland

Bill Kelly, now with Keller Online, remembered one time when two people in the same office got bigger tops. "The office wasn't even big enough, but they had to have their new tops," he recalled.

Terry did not expect to make his career solely at Keller. It was, when he first arrived, more of a "stopping place" before he would return to the East Coast. "But, it was a young company and we were getting in on the ground floor. There were all sorts of opportunities. When I saw the potential growth of the company, I thought the opportunities seemed unlimited."

Supporting the Associates

As a company, Keller was family-oriented. There were many social activities involving the whole family — picnics, associate teams for basketball, volleyball, and other events. Keller even had a championship men's softball team that Jim Keller played on from 1972 until the league folded in 1997.

There were dinners with Jack and Ethel. "It was not unusual for my wife and me to dine with Jack and Ethel twice a year," Mark remembered.

"The four of us would go out to dinner and to the theater," Terry said. "In the 1970s, he took us to Milwaukee for an overnight weekend, including dinner and lodging. It was pretty cool to do this with the president of the company."

Mark Tremble hits one out of the park at a company picnic: late-1970s

"I'll always look back on this place with a lot of fun memories," Terry said.

The bond grew between associates because not only did they work hard together, they played hard. Picnics, holiday parties, sports teams, and more were all opportunities to socialize outside of work. Sometimes families spent weekends or vacations together. "We did a lot of things together outside of work," Jan Reh Hamblin said.

Chapter 7

Product Development

While growth in government regulations created demand for Keller to develop new products and services, how did it know what to develop? "Our sales people would go to our customers and solicit ideas," Bob said. "Some 2,000 to 3,000 product ideas have come from our customers. We are sensitive to our customers' needs and issues."

As a young man, Bob often traveled with his father to meet with customers. Naturally, they'd have their product line with them, as well as certain items they wanted to discuss with a client.

"Our customers would redirect us," he said. "One time we went to Milwaukee and started talking about some kind of training product. We ended up getting an idea from the customer for a manual on how to use OSHA signs for workplace hazard identification. We started with one train of thought and when we finished, we came away with a different solution, a different product. Then we'd test the idea and it was almost always a better solution."

Jim agreed. "We're not interested in solving our needs. We are interested in solving the customers' needs."

It is because of that business philosophy that 80 to 90 percent of Keller's products and services have been successful. "We've had some perfect failures, though," Bob added.

They've learned from their mistakes. For example, in the early 1990s, they initiated a fee-based telephone service. Customers weren't interested. But that concept was the embryo for

The Keller Technical Institute (KTI) is an educational unit of J.J. Keller & Associates, Inc. which presents training seminars, both nation-wide and at the home office in Neenah. These seminars provide information on current regulatory changes and compliance issues, as well as how to deal with day-to-day challenges through industry best practices. Key issues covered include DOT and OSHA compliance, hazardous materials transportation, transport security, and workplace safety management.

KellerOnline®, a successful Internet-based service that was launched in 2002.

Another mistake was a driver handbook that became so unwieldy at more than 600 pages that the cost was too high. Nobody bought it. "We designed a chicken and ended up with a turkey. It was not developed methodically," Bob said. "Now we have research-aided design. When we consider a product, we have a vision statement and marketing statement for it. It gives the product a rudder."

Customer opinions are very important in the development process. Customers recognize value when they see it and reject products that don't have value. "Once the customer recognizes value, it doesn't matter where the product is in our catalog, he or she will find it," Bob said.

Bob describes the company as "an edger." "We are a little bit on the edge, exploring the edge. That is how we built the business, snooping around the next corner to see what's there."

Keller Factoid ...

1981 –
- Keller offered over 600 different items in its product line.
- The Wang computer equipment was installed, and payroll was the first system implemented.
- Keller's first catalog, *Fleet Forms & Supplies Catalog*, containing over 200 items, was produced.
- *Bertha*, a 13-speed tandem-axle diesel truck with a 22-foot box, was added to the Keller fleet.
- Keller was granted its first patent for a new design of a lightweight polycarbonate holder to display hazardous material placards.

1982 –
- The first computerized photo-typesetter, with a speed of over 150 lines per minute, was installed in the composition department.
- Roadway Express, the largest common carrier in the country, purchased 50,000 logbooks each year from Keller.

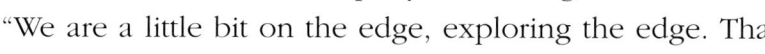

Jack Keller is still peeking around the corners, looking for the next deal, as Bill Kelly, a 26-year veteran of the company learned in the early 1990s. He was called into Jack's office for a talk about something that could be big, really big.

"Jack said, 'The Internet: I don't know what it is, but I know it's going to be very big,'" Bill recalled. "He said, 'I want you to build one just like it, but not quite the same.' I nodded my head and said I'd work on it."

That story is pure Jack Keller. At a point in his life when most men his age had left the office behind, Jack saw the future for many more Keller products to come.

Betty Backman and Amy Vanden Oever with a product display: 1985

Marne, who worked in the Keller technical library as a young girl, moved into market research after college. In those early years, she sometimes looked at "oddball things," some of which came to fruition and others that had very short lives.

Marne earned her undergraduate degree in international relations and business from the University of Wisconsin-Oshkosh and a master's degree in organizational leadership and quality from Marian College in Fond du Lac. Today, as corporate strategic planning manager, she focuses primarily on corporate and strategic planning through investigation of new product lines and market areas.

Ideas come from many different places, including Grandpa Jack. "I still get handwritten notes and articles from him," Marne said. "He will never entirely let go."

While Jack is semi-retired as chairman, he keeps his many files of ideas, adding to them constantly. Coming into the office quite frequently, he said, "Still got the old brain going. I'd rather be active until I'm gone, than just idle away my time."

Mostly, though, new products are developed through careful design. "Now, we are very process and policy-oriented. We talk to the customers. Whenever we look at anything new, we go out in the field, involve customers in product development and in reviewing the product," she said.

The Product Development Process consists of seven phases:

1. Identify a product area, using a variety of sources for ideas.
2. Identify concepts to test, looking at research to determine the market for different product concepts.
3. Conduct research, including assembling articles, government information, and industry news.
4. Create a project outline, including an outline of issues the product should cover.
5. Identify resources that will be needed for the project, including team members and material specifications.
6. Produce the product, incorporating formal and informal comments and feedback as it is developed.
7. Periodically review feedback on the product and realign it to meet customer needs.

Keller has a culture that encourages creativity, introducing 30 to 50 new products each year. "We have product ideas that are developed centrally or corporately, and others that evolve from a specific business unit or profit center," Bob said.

One of the goals, in fact, is for each of the nine profit centers to develop what the company refers to as "top line solutions." "We can't grow as a company with $30,000 to $50,000-a-year products or product extensions. These top line solutions are products or services with significant revenue potential," Bob said.

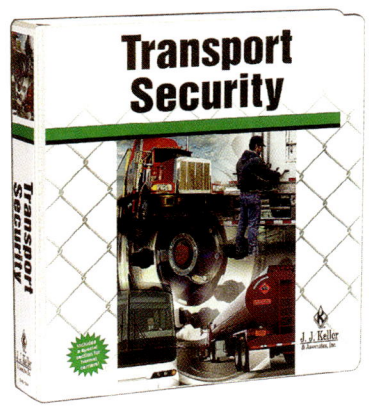

Research and development is geared now to creating whole new product lines for areas like human resources, food safety, and transportation security. All are completely new product lines for Keller. Realizing that the world turned on a dime on September 11, 2001, the company also is working extensively on solutions for site security and disaster planning.

"The big change is that we now live in an era of terrorism and global uncertainty," Bob said. "The fact is, the landscape has changed forever. Our environment since 9/11 is fundamentally different — a new world order."

To meet the new challenges, Keller has to be aggressive, but fiscally conservative. The emphasis has to continue to be on superior value. Bob commented, "We cannot raise prices by much, so we have to add value to differentiate ourselves."

New Technologies

For a company that has its origins in print media, Keller has not been afraid to move into new technologies — video, software, and Internet-based services, for example.

In a 1995 interview with the Appleton Post-Crescent about the company's new online presence, Bob said he was doubtful at first about whether the new technologies would work for his company. Then he saw a demonstration of the prototype for a Keller software product to teach workers about OSHA's hazardous materials regulations and test their knowledge and application of the information. "It knocked my socks off," he said.

While some in the company questioned whether these new technologies would hurt print publication sales, Keller has found companies buying both print materials and computer-based Keller-Soft® software products or training videos. Always believing in "value-added" products, Keller also offers customization of virtually all its products, from a company logo on a handbook to complete integration of a sophisticated, new safety program into corporate policies and procedures manuals.

"I think one of the best things we've done is to compete with ourselves," Bob said in the Post-Crescent interview. "If you can improve the product, reduce the price and still make money, everybody wins."

Viewed from left to right, Keller catalogs throughout the years

KellerOnline® and Web-based Services

One of the major new areas for development is *KellerOnline*® (KOL), which brings many services into one convenient online location, complete with immediate customer assistance.

Rustin, Bob and Lynne's son, joined the company to develop KOL. It was Jim Keller who announced to the company that Keller was bringing in "a hotshot from GE" to create *KellerOnline*®, Rustin said. "The bar was set very high."

Rustin said they spent three weeks on the road just talking to customers about whether the concept had any merit. *KellerOnline*® is designed to help safety professionals get beyond compliance by integrating OSHA, DOT, and EPA regulations and compliance documents with news, safety information, online discussions, personal assistance, and interactive tools. Those using the service through a monthly subscription can cross-reference chemicals, write a safety plan, perform an audit, create a training session, or discuss best practices with industry peers. The KOL personal assistant service is also available to answer online compliance questions.

The beta test for the new product, which took $1.5 million in development costs, was launched the week before Rustin was married in September 2000. "It went up while I was on my honeymoon," he said.

After the three-month beta test, KOL went live in January 2001. Most gratifying to Rustin is that 80 percent of the subscribers renew. "We just crossed the 7,000 subscriber mark — with our long-term goal still to reach 20,000," Rustin said.

KOL has little competition because it is so comprehensive. "It's the only safety management tool that integrates all aspects of the safety management process. It's the leading service for safety professionals," Rustin said.

KOL is not Keller's only entry into web-based services. The company has a development group creating services like *Driver Management Online*™, which lets transport companies conduct many key tasks more efficiently, including maintaining driver qualification files, managing alcohol and drug testing, hiring new employees, recording accidents, monitoring training programs, and reporting compliance and management information. Subscribers can use *Driver Management Online*™ to search for qualified

Keller Factoid ...

1983 –
- Keller employed 280 associates.
- Net sales reached $10,527,448.
- Central Distribution Services (CDS) was established to provide warehousing and storage space, shipping, receiving, and material handling services to outside customers.

1984 –
- Customer service/sales hit its first departmental "million dollar month."
- Sales order number 300,000 was entered into the computer system.
- The bindery team produced 826,000 logbooks — an 83% increase over December 1983.

drivers, to bring driver qualification files up to date, and to integrate third-party information, like background checks or drug and alcohol checks, with other confidential records to increase efficiency.

Food Safety

With the U.S. Government's Center for Disease Control and Prevention estimating that foodborne diseases cause 76 million illnesses, 325,000 hospitalizations, and 5,000 deaths each year in this country, the need to protect the food chain from the farm to the table cannot be overstated. With the additional worry in the post-9/11 era that a terrorist attack might jeopardize the nation's food supply, manufacturers and processors need practical tools to help them keep up with food safety regulations and education for their employees.

Keller products include the *Compliance Manual for Food Quality and Safety*, which provides "how to comply" explanations for critical U.S. Department of Agriculture and Food and Drug Administration (FDA) regulations. A food security chapter offers advice to help safeguard property, personnel, and product.

Other food safety products include *A Recipe for Food Safety Success*, which is designed to give employees an understanding of the "big picture" regarding food safety and cleanliness; *Employee's Guide to Food Safety*, a training program; *Food Safety for Foodservice: An Employee Video Series*; and *Food Safety Handbook for Foodservice Employees*.

"We want to not only help companies comply with regulations, but have best practices," Marne said. "The food safety security issue in this country is huge."

One of the major pushes for food safety products comes from the FDA's food safety program called "Hazard Analysis and Critical Control Points," or HACCP. It requires manufacturers to analyze hazards; identify critical control points in production; and establish preventive measures with critical limits and monitoring procedures for each control point, corrective actions when a critical limit is not met, and verifications. It also requires recordkeeping.

One of the advantages of these food safety products is that it allows Keller entry into the major food production companies that, in the past, may not have needed Keller products other than for their transportation departments. Once a food safety relationship is established, other regulatory and safety needs emerge.

Human Resources

Clearly, Keller operates very differently today than in the 1950s and 1960s. "In the '50s and maybe even the '60s you could be very cavalier in your business. If you didn't like the way somebody was doing his or her work, you could simply say 'you're fired,'" Ron Phillips said. "Or, you could pick out somebody and say 'you're promoted.' It was that innocent back then."

Bob agrees. "We operated consistent with that era. There wasn't a lot of efficiency in small companies at that time."

Words once used with complete freedom in everyday business are now viewed as not "politically correct" or even considered a form of harassment. Codes of conduct have been established to ensure a business culture that is very positive. And, these rules and regulations related to human resources not only make for a better working environment for workers who once may have suffered in silence, they are also business opportunities for Keller.

Human resources products, in fact, are a strong new product line for the company. Among these products are Keller's *HR Orientation for Employees*

Viewed from left to right, Keller direct mail has come a long way through the years.

Training Program; *Human Resources Training Customizer Software*; *FMLA Revealed: A Step by Step Approach Manual*; *FMLA Manager Software*; and *State Labor Law Poster Kits.*

"Managing and administering the Family Medical Leave Act (FMLA) can be a real headache for companies," Marne said. "We have high hopes that this product line will be quite helpful."

Hard Work

Yes, there are opportunities to be creative and explore new areas of interest at J. J. Keller & Associates, Inc., but make no mistake — product development is primarily hard work. "We are not big on talking about it. We are big on doing it," Bob said. "Product development is exciting and motivating; but fundamentally, it is a lot of hard work."

There are times that a tremendous amount of work goes into a concept, only to have it shelved for five to 10 years. "Its time may not have come yet," Bob said. "Then one day, the time is right, the product comes out, and it is a success for us."

Keller is not like a university think tank where people get paid for dreaming up ideas. According to Bob, "Our strength is in operations, excelling in creating new products through a lot of hard work, research, and tweaking. It really takes a lot of discipline and persistence."

Bob, Jack, and Jim at the groundbreaking ceremony for a Vinland addition: 1978

Chapter 8

Responding to Regulations

Keller now has thousands of products all responding to government regulations, many more if product customization is considered. But where did all those regulations come from? Most people would suspect it was Congress writing them, but that was and is not true, according to Bob Keller.

Government regulations proliferated through the Executive Branch of the federal government. Cabinet-level departments like the Department of Transportation, the Department of Health and Human Services, the Department of Labor, the Environmental Protection Agency, and agencies like the Occupational Safety and Health Administration and the Federal Highway Administration create these rules.

"Regulations now deal with just about everything that people do," Bob said. "Regulation is good for us, but excess regulation isn't good for the country."

In the 1980s, there were so many regulatory initiatives that Keller had dozens of major product initiatives on its plate at the same time.

"In the period of the Clinton Administration, there was not much activity, but we are beginning to see it again in the [George W.] Bush Administration. Most regulation comes during Republican administrations, not Democratic. You can see it more with the Reagan and Bush Senior Administrations than with Clinton," Bob said.

Jim agreed. "Homeland Security was created because of 9/11. That happened to be when Bush was in office, but it's all tied to more regulation and bigger government."

While regulators may get carried away at times, "they possibly have saved thousands of lives," Jim said. "It's hard to put a price on that."

Regulation Milestones

- **1970** Department of Transportation (DOT) established safety regulations related to driver qualification which required about 20 different pieces of paperwork on the driver, his or her activities, and the vehicles driven. Keller has developed about 100 different products in response to these regulations. Among the most recent is *Driver Management Online*™ released in 2002, which is designed to help companies deal with recordkeeping, along with the growing shortage of qualified drivers. The concept is that every tool a business would need to recruit and screen drivers, including access to alcohol testing reports, is available to companies for a monthly fee. "We expect 200,000 drivers to use this service within two years," Bob said.

Keller Factoid ...

1985 –
- The company had over 1,300 services clients, and over 51,000 customers.
- 80 five-drawer file cabinets held customer files for the sales department.
- The printing team went over the million impression mark in one day for the first time operating three web presses and eight sheet presses.

1986 –
- The screen printing department was established, enabling the printing of vinyl placards and trailer signs.
- Product sales hit the two million dollar mark for the first time.
- Distribution hit a monthly shipping record when 7,641 shipments of stock orders were sent out.

- **1977** DOT established the hazardous materials regulations, which completely revamped the shipping and handling of hazardous materials. Keller has created hundreds of products, including how-to-comply manuals and signage for trucks. The company is now serving as a consultant to airlines, reviewing policies, products, and staff training related to hazardous materials.

- **1984** The Environmental Protection Agency issued hazardous waste regulations related to the identification, storage, distribution, and disposal of hazardous waste products.

- **1986** Employee's right to know, issued by the Occupational Safety and Health Administration (OSHA), guarantees that employees understand the properties and potential safety and health hazards of substances they may be exposed to in the workplace. With around 1,000 pages of OSHA workplace safety regulations to work from, Keller has developed hundreds of compliance and training products.

- **1989** DOT drug testing regulations, which require alcohol and other drug testing of commercial drivers, airplane pilots, railroad workers, mass transit, and pipeline and commercial vessel operators, among others. The company has produced hundreds of products for recordkeeping and training for the transportation industry.

- **1990 to today** Food safety, from farm to the table; OSHA regulations governing the construction industry; DOT regulations governing hazardous materials and hours-of-service; security; and human resources.

All of these regulatory thrusts have an impact on businesses that are already challenged in a difficult economy.

"When the government comes in and checks on a company, it doesn't expect perfection," Jim said. "It expects things to be moving in the right direction and an honest attempt to meet basic regulations."

Going Metric and Other Great Ideas

Over the years, Mark Tremble frequently found himself hearing many of the ideas that Jack developed, including some that, frankly, "the boys" simply ignored. "Jack was certainly the entrepreneur type who needed people to get his ideas going. I happened to be one of those people he constantly told about his ideas. Sometimes the boys wouldn't want to do them, but Jack wanted to. I would try to get at least half of them done," Mark said.

Among the ideas were travel and trade products, such as passport holders, coffee cups, and luggage. One idea that was clearly ahead of its time was bottled water from Poygan Springs, a body of water not far from Jack's cottage in central Wisconsin. Bottled water could easily fall in the same "if only" file as the tape on sanitary napkins of 20 years earlier.

"He had every idea under the sun," Terry Quirk said. "In fact, we have Jack's research and development files archived in storage. Each of the 300 to 400 files contains one to two sheets of information — it's amazing we still have them all."

"He is a man who, no matter what he is thinking, reading, or watching, continues to visualize concepts," Mark said. "He is brilliant, and just a bit off the wall. The success of this company shows you what determination and hard work can do."

One reason he had so many ideas is that Jack was always incredibly well-read. Even at age 84, he reads six newspapers a day.

> **Remember when . . .**
>
> ... Bob Keller turned 50, and he called me into his office for a discussion. What he wanted to talk about was that back in the early days when I was hired, Bob had thought it unusual that the company would hire "such an old man." Bob couldn't help but comment how one's perspective changes over the years, as I was 50 when hired.
>
> – George McDowell (Retired) Editorial Resources

In the 1970s and early 1980s, Jack recognized a movement afoot to correct the fact that the United States was the only industrialized nation in the world that did not use the metric system as its predominant system of measurement.

In order to encourage the change to metric, Keller adopted a practice begun in New Zealand and picked up in this country in the state of Massachusetts — naming a "Little Miss" or "Master Metric," someone who ideally would live his or her whole life in a metric world. As a headline in the Oshkosh Daily Northwestern put it, "Little Miss Metric is a symbol of impending change." Keller's Little Miss Metric weighed in at 4.1 kilograms and measured 49.5 centimeters.

Pat Laux, who was then general editor for metric publications for Keller, including *The Modernized Metric System Explained*, said in the Northwestern interview, "If New Zealanders, Australians, and Canadians can switch over, why can't we in the United States? But it should be done in a specified period of time. If we drag on, still using highway signs, for instance, that indicate miles and kilometers, most people will look only at the miles. We have to do a complete turnover."

The U.S. Metric Conversion Board was considered so ineffective in this country that it was disestablished in the fall of 1982. Congress tried again in

1988, using the Omnibus Trade and Competitive Act of 1988, to designate the metric system as the preferred system of weights and measures for U.S. trade and commerce.

Federal agencies now are required to use the metric system in procurement, grants, and other business-related activities. Advocates of the metric system continue to argue, as Jack does, that the nation's industry and economy are handicapped by our reluctance to join the rest of the world.

Jack believes the failure to adopt the metric system was really the government's recognition that it would cost a fortune because everything in our lives would have to be remeasured, particularly the distances between places in this vast country. "They couldn't figure out how they would remeasure all of the U.S. territory when they didn't even have it all in feet and inches," he said.

While the rest of the world doubted the U.S. would ever convert completely, there were true believers like Jack who kept the metric dream alive. He had, in fact, spent about a half million company dollars to create a variety of references on the metric system in the 1970s. There was a five-volume set that comprised the *Metric System Guide Library*, which was proudly described in the fall 1974 issue of the *Circle K Roundup*, the associate newsletter. "This is the only definitive metric reference series in America, and has been judged by experts to be the most comprehensive metric information from a single source," it was reported.

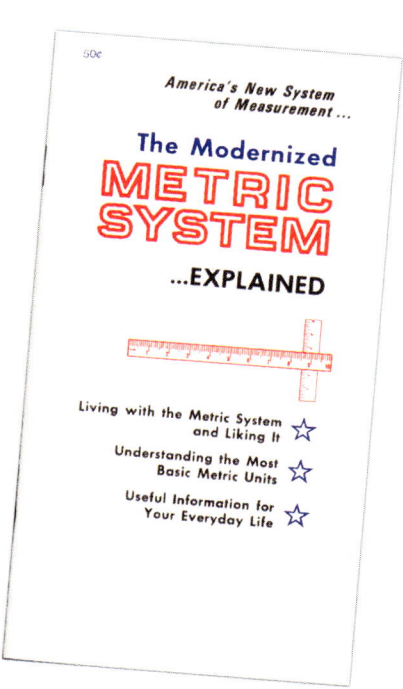

The library consisted of these volumes: *Metrication in the United States, Legislation and Regulatory Controls, Metric Units Edition, Reference Sources,* and *Metric Definitions.* Keller also developed semi-annual update subscriptions for these five guides.

The winter 1974-75 *Circle K Roundup* announced publication of the *Metrication Handbook* which "will help you start 'thinking metric' by seeing the simplicity of the system in relation to our present customary system of measure." But, the largest-selling product was a 36-page pamphlet, *The Modernized Metric System Explained*, written by Jack and edited by Pat Laux.

"The International Metric Association found it to be the most practical guide for the public in the metric world," Jack said. "It was a good idea and it worked."

Little Miss Metric is symbo[l]

By ANDREA BLETZINGER
Of the Women's Staff

NEENAH — The change to metric measurement in the United States is a slow, sometimes haphazard procedure.

Signs along highways give kilometers as well as miles. Measuring articles such as cups for cooking, tapes for measuring and scales are marked in liters, centimeters and kilograms as well as ounces, inches and pounds.

But so far the general public has not taken readily to the metric system.

To present the idea in an appealing manner several communities in Massachusetts have adopted a Little Miss or Master Metric. Locally J. J. Keller and Associates have named tiny Sarah Sue Wendt, born July 12, as their Miss Metric. She is the daughter of Sue and Jim Wendt, 744 Warsaw St., Menasha. Mrs. Wendt is a former employe of J. J. Keller.

Sarah Sue wieghed 4.1 kg (kilograms) and measured 49.5 cm (centimeters) at birth.

Pat Laux, general editor for metric publications for the company, explained that the idea came from New Zealand. George and Elspeth Preddey had announced the birth of their daughter Jean in a New Zealand newspaper and included her weight in the announcement — 3.17 kg.

The Metric Advisory Board of New Zealand promptly "adopted" her as Little Miss Metric. They have followed her growth, annually publishing her weight and height in the papers, always in metric numbers. Jean is now in first grade, and her whole class

Pat Laux

has been adopted by New Zealand Metric Advisory Board!

In the six years of young Jean Preddey's life New Zealand has gone to the metric system.

"We have a bill passed by Congress in December 1975 authorizing use of the metric system in this country and establishing a metric board to oversee the transition," Miss Laux said.

"But the nominees to the board made by President Gerald Ford were not approved by the Senate; they just didn't find time to do it.

"Now President Carter is re-examining the list which includes several nominated by Ford. Congress can take no action until the list is announced."

Four years ago Pat Laux began her own work with metrics. In 1974 she edited a small booklet — "The Modernized Metric System.. Explained" — published by J. J. Keller and Associates. It was designed to be a handout for schools nd industry, but the publishers decided to place it on sale at Kmarts across the country.

The response was far beyond their expectations, and sales of the little book are now in the second million.

"I have been invited to speak for several groups in the area on the metric system," Miss Laux said. "Already I have two talks scheduled for this fall, and I'm willing to travel within a 50 mile radius to talk about metrics.

"If New Zealanders, Australians and Canadians can switch over, why can't we in the United States? But it should be done in a specified period of time. If we drag on, still using highway signs, for instance, that indicate both miles and kilometers, most people will look only at the miles. We have to do a complete turnover."

To facilitate a change in highway habits, stickers indicating metric mileage can be applied to speedometers of cars.

"General Motors has almost completely gone into the metric system," Miss Laux said. "Companies supplying GM with such things as screws, nuts and bolts, are also going to the metric system, and the other large auto manufacturers are following suit. 1980 is the goal year for GM."

Another business group that have actually welcomed the change to metric are the distilleries and wineries. Their products are in competition with those of other countries in which the bottle measure is in liters. Many wineries are already in metric measured bottles.

"Once the change is made, there is no turning back. In the auto industry the tooling alone to go on the metric system costs thousands of dollars. They don't want to switch back."

Another area of change is already visible — Celcius temperature. Television weathercasts and the signboards on banks give both Celcius and Fahrenheit degrees.

"Canadians were treated to a large advertisement in April 1975 — 'Say good night to Fahrenheit' — and the temperatures were given only in Celcius from then on!" Miss Laux related.

She noted that school children are aware and using the metric system.

"People seem to think it will be difficult," she said. "When someone wonders about using a different method of measuring, I ask them if they can tell me how many teaspoons are in a tablespoon or ounces in a cup.

"In most audiences there are few who can reply. People rely on charts. It would be the same with changing to the metric system. A few simple keys will help."

In the metric booklet Pat Laux offered three simple "handles" to learning the metric system.

"Remember that a meter is a yard, plus a little extra. A kilogram is two pounds, plus a little extra. A liter is a quart, plus a little extra.. .The metric measures are close enough to what you are using now, so you won't have a big problem in adjusting your mental measuring stick."

In the spring 1976 issue of the *Circle K Roundup*, an article on the pamphlet carried the headline, "Read Any Best-Sellers Lately?" The article was delightful in retrospect:

> "In trade book publishing, books such as *Helter Skelter*, etc., are considered best sellers when they reach 20,000 copies in sales in their original edition. The paperback editions are best sellers when a half million or so are sold. By these guidelines (or any guidelines), J. J. Keller has a runaway best seller in *The Modernized Metric System Explained*. In March alone, more than 50,000 copies of this 36-page consumer-oriented booklet were shipped all over the U.S. While the majority of them have gone to bookstores and other retail outlets such as Kmart and Treasure Island, these are by no means our only customers. A Green Bay savings and loan has bought 10,000 copies as a premium giveaway, a major

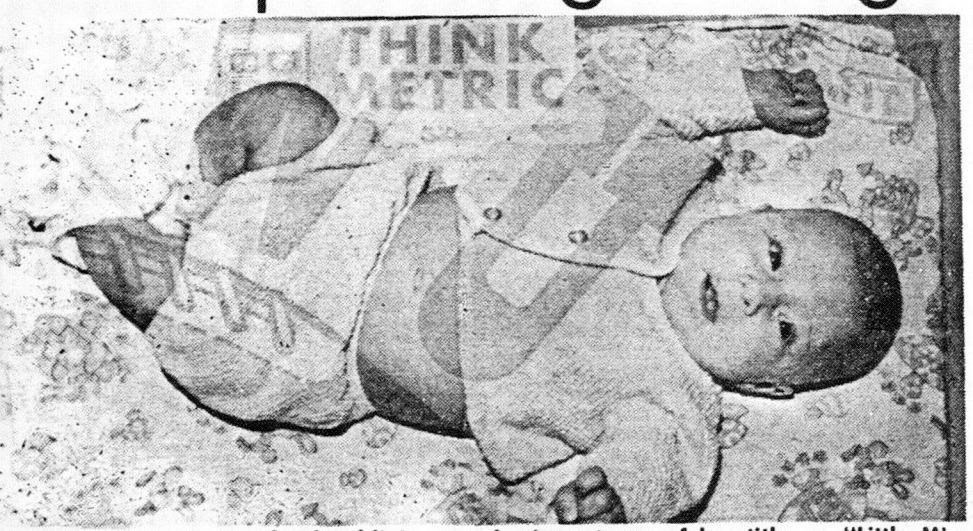

Sarah Sue Wendt is completely oblivious to the importance of her title — "Little Miss Metric." She is the daughter of Mr. and Mrs. James Wendt, 755 Warsaw St., Menasha.

Pat Laux was interviewed by the Oshkosh Daily Northwestern in this 1977 article about "Little Miss Metric."

oil company purchased a like number for employee education, and a leading correspondence school did likewise for use in its study courses. Thousands of elementary and high school students throughout America are getting their introduction to the metric system from this remarkable booklet.

More than one-million copies are now in print, and as everyone knows, the second million comes easier. Quite a success story — and not a page of sex or violence in the whole book!"

The second million was not quite as easy as the newsletter writer suggested. With many copies in stock, it was Mark Tremble's job to push this 50-cent pamphlet to the general public. He went from store to store to stock it as an impulse item at the checkout counters at discount houses like ShopKo, Kmart, True Value Hardware, Treasure Island, and Prange Way.

"The boss said fill up the van and don't come back until they're all sold," he recalled. "I would get in the van and drive to as many stores as it would take to sell those books. I would go in and say 'I have a great book you should sell.'"

Roughly 600,000 of the pamphlets were sold by his leaving 1,000 to 2,000 copies at each store.

Mark remembers these business trips, which were as far away as Ohio, as an especially difficult time because he and his wife, Debbie, had just had a baby who was colicky. "I would drive off in the van filled with these pamphlets on Sunday night and not get back until the following Friday."

Aerial view of the Vinland complex: late-1980s

Chapter 9

A Part of the Family

Foxy

When Lynn "Foxy" Fox joined Keller in 1975, gross sales were about $2 million. The company did not have a formal human resources department, so he began helping out in a number of associate services areas.

Over the last 11 years, Lynn has worked directly with Jack Keller, serving as special programs administrator. That role has involved traveling with the Kellers as well as helping them with a variety of projects. "Jack has so many facets to his life. He's a very diversified man, with many different

Lynn Fox at the downtown office: 1977

businesses," Lynn said. "He works on 10 different projects at the same time. That's just the way he is."

Lynn may know the Kellers better than anyone because he has spent so much time with them. "Even though he is a visionary man, I don't think Jack had a vision for what he thought this company would become," Lynn said. "Jack never dreamed that the company would become responsible for 950 associates and their families."

Lynn sees Jack as being a big burly guy with a rough and often-raised voice, but a "puppy dog inside even though he doesn't want to show it."

He also calls Ethel Keller, "a wonderful individual. She is the backbone of the family. She is very intelligent and has an extremely good sense of humor."

Keller Factoid ...

1987 –
- Keller had over 430 associates.
- The first Keller training videos hit the market.
- A new Apollo web offset duplicator press was installed to use for short-run logbook orders.

1988 –
- Construction began on a 40,000 square-foot addition to expand the distribution operations.
- *Reg-A-Dex®* was issued, Keller's first publication-on-disk.
- The 401(k) plan began. The first company match deposited into the program was $76,000 in 1989.
- With the addition of a second Wang 7310 computer, Keller had the largest Wang installation north of Milwaukee, Wisconsin.

Mary Murvine

When Mary Murvine was first hired to work at Keller in 1977, she was given a message she never forgot: "Stick around kid. This will really pay off for you." Two weeks later, she was moved into the position of executive secretary. Now corporate secretary and administrative officer, she has never looked back.

"It was such a little company in the beginning and so rollicking here. The personalities were so strong," she said.

Loyalty to the place where you work has been a part of her family's makeup. "I come from a history of people who stayed a long time at their respective companies. You did your job and stayed," she said.

Keller, which had about 140 associates when Mary arrived, was so much better than the job she had before she took time off to raise her son. "I had an opportunity to learn about anything that happened at this company. Jack Keller was the kind of guy who explained everything that was happening and why. He was a mentor because he wanted me to know everything,"

Mary and Jack at the downtown office: 1979

Mary said. "I am like a sponge. I'm not an expert on anything, but I know a lot about everything we do."

Her job includes managing the executive office and administrative staff. She also is corporate secretary on the Board of Directors, where she is a member and handles the minutes. "It's always been interesting. I never know what I'll do next," she said. "I am so personally entwined with the family. It's just always so interesting, there's always something new and new opportunities."

Bob believes Mary was instrumental in the company's growth and development. "She's really smart and she's had a lot of experience," he said. "She's worked her whole life in executive support capacities."

While Mary has no immediate plans to retire, Bob knows she will be very hard to replace. "When people like her leave, you usually have to replace them with two or three people or delegate to two or three different areas," he said. "She is unique."

Frank Pelisek

Frank "Jack" Pelisek was a bit brusque, gruff, but incredibly bright, "a walking encyclopedia about the law," Mary Murvine recalls. "He was a tremendous resource."

Jack, who was corporate counsel and served on the Keller Board of Directors from 1980 until his death in June 2002, "was a wonderful man. To outsiders he could appear cold and tough, though he was a pussycat inside," Mary added.

A longtime partner with the Michael, Best, & Friedrich legal firm of Milwaukee, "Jack provided a lot of broad-based experience and wisdom," Bob said. "He had a no-nonsense style, but was not political. These qualities allowed Jack to provide objective insight and guidance to the corporation over many years."

Frank "Jack" Pelisek

Jack counseled and repeatedly encouraged Keller to become an "S" corporation, which allows it to be treated like a partnership for taxation purposes, a benefit over the standard corporation.

Following Jack's illness and death, John Sapp (a senior partner at the law firm) has served as corporate counsel and filled his open spot on the Board of Directors.

Chapter 10

Giving Back to the Community

It was on Ethel Keller's 70th birthday in 1991 that Jack gave her a gift that she treasures most of all — creation of the Keller Foundation, Ltd. A woman whose heart really is in doing good deeds for the community, she was thrilled that the foundation would make it even easier to support the many good works that the company and the Keller family had already been doing.

There's no question there were tax advantages, something that Jack especially appreciates. It will help the family avoid the so-called "death tax," meaning the inheritance tax, which, at the time, they estimated could eat away 45 percent of their business assets.

Jack and Ethel, Bob, Jim, and Bob's children, Marne and Rustin, have maximum control over the foundation and how it will give away the money. After Jack and Ethel's deaths, the children and grandchildren will administer the fund.

In addition to the Keller Foundation, Ltd., the Kellers have been quite generous to the Community Foundation for the Fox Valley Region, Inc. In 1994, they gifted 200,000 shares of J. J. Keller & Associates, Inc. stock and another 150,000 shares in 1998. To date, the Kellers have given more than $9 million to the Community Foundation.

While about $2.5 million has been contributed to the Keller Foundation, Ltd., the balance of the estate of Jack and Ethel will be principally assigned to the Keller Foundation, Ltd. after their deaths.

Why not leave all their money to their children? The donor-advised fund and the Keller Foundation, Ltd. reflect the senior Kellers' philosophy. Not only does the couple not want to give the government their hard-earned dollars, they don't want to take away the incentive for future generations of Kellers to work as hard as they did to establish their wealth.

It's important to recognize that their children and grandchildren have a secure future, thanks to Keller stock. Beyond that, Jack and Ethel believe that too much wealth handed to these younger generations would be unhealthy.

In an article in *Foundation Focus*, a publication of the Community Foundation, Jack echoed that philosophy by saying, "Over-indulging heirs is not good. Why create a group of people who don't have to work and have no respect for money?"

A partial list of donations given on behalf of J. J. Keller & Associates, Inc. includes:

- $500,000 to Theda Clark Medical Center for a trauma center room.
- $500,000 to Rawhide Boys Ranch for a high school.
- $400,000 to the Fox Valley Technical College for a truck driving range.
- $250,000 to the Boy Scouts to create a volunteer area and a naturalist area at their new service center.
- $200,000 to the Fox Cities Children's Museum for the Starship Discovery exhibit.
- $200,000 to St. Gabriel's Parish for a childhood center and carport.
- $150,000 to the Fox River Area Girl Scouts for a volunteer center and an outdoor learning courtyard.
- $150,000 to the Boy Scouts to build Fort Keller at Camp Rokilio.
- $140,000 to Monte Alverno Retreat Center for an elevator.
- $120,000 to Park View Health Center for two courtyards and a beauty/barbershop.
- $100,000 to the Fox Cities Performing Arts Center for the information booth.
- $100,000 to the Boys and Girls Club to develop a Big Brothers/Big Sisters office.
- $100,000 to Lutheran Homes of Oshkosh for a courtyard.
- $75,000 to the Neenah Library to fund the building of the lobby.
- $75,000 to the Menasha Library to fund the building of the lobby.

Due to an increasing need to provide comprehensive educational services to youths at **Rawhide Boys Ranch**, Jack and Ethel gifted funds to construct **Starr Academy**, a large educational facility. The new school, located in New London, was dedicated in October 1998.

The **Winneconne Municipal Center** was made possible with a generous gift from Jack and Ethel. The facility houses the municipal offices, police department, library, chamber office, and a Winnebago watershed exhibit. Construction began in 1998, and the new building was dedicated in September 1999.

In 1999, Jack and Ethel provided funding for the development of the **Starship Discovery - Mission Earth** exhibit at the **Fox Cities Children's Museum** in Appleton. The exhibit features an alien space craft studying the earth, providing children the opportunity to learn more about the geography of our planet, different people and cultures around the world, and the solar system.

In 1995, the Bay-Lakes Council of the Boy Scouts of America developed a cub scout overnight camp program, and identified Camp Rokilio, located in Kiel, as a suitable building site. Jack and Ethel provided funds for **Fort Keller at Camp Rokilio**, which can house 32 scouts and 10 parents/leaders.

Jack and Ethel provided funding for the development of the **Ceil Courtois Courtyard** at Park View Health Center in Winnebago following the tremendous success of the **Stephen Courtois Courtyard** at the same facility. Both courtyards provide wheelchair access, comfortable seating, beautiful gardens, and a water feature and feeders to attract birds and butterflies for the enjoyment of the residents.

In 1996, Neenah voters approved the construction of an all-new **Neenah Public Library**. Jack and Ethel provided a grant for the main lobby of the facility. Construction of the two-story structure with approximately 40,000 square feet commenced in 1999, and the new building was dedicated in 2000.

All paintings by Bob Locke

"We like doing projects that otherwise wouldn't get done," Ethel said. "Acquiring money was never my goal in life, but I've since learned you can do wonderful things with it. There's more satisfaction knowing someone in need has gotten $1,000 than my spending $1,000 on me."

The Kellers have also set up these additional funds through the Community Foundation

- An emergency fund at Community Clinic for individuals who find they cannot afford a specific test or treatment. Several hundred people have benefited from it in the last five years.

- An emergency fund in Appleton at the Fox Valley Family Practice for those needing psychiatric treatment.

- An adaptive medical equipment fund for children with disabilities through ThedaCare.

"It's my missionary instinct," Ethel said. "Originally, I wanted to be a missionary."

The couple also gives away money now, rather than waiting for their deaths, because they enjoy seeing the end results. They have money to share because of their business success and have lived modestly throughout

Dedication of Rawhide High School funded by Jack and Ethel: 1998
(Pictured with Jack and Ethel are Bart and Cherry Starr, and Jan and John Gillespie, the founders of Rawhide Boys Ranch.)

the years. "We don't live any differently now than we did then," Jack said.

"We have lived in the same house for 43 years," Ethel agreed. "I was raised poor. My mom was one of 12 on a farm with no electricity."

In a 2001 interview, Larry Kath, President and Chief Executive Officer of the Community Foundation, described Jack as "a really special guy for a lot of reasons. He's a very generous individual. Both he and Ethel want to help people who have not had the opportunities they had."

Giving away money is in many ways like earning it, according to Jack. It offends him when they make a sizable gift to an organization and, instead of a thank you, receive a request for more money. "You will find greedy people," he said.

Despite the challenges, the Kellers are proud to be able to give back to help others. "There's satisfaction in knowing that I am doing what I think is right," Ethel said.

Keller Factoid ...

1989 –
- Keller had over 530 associates.
- The company was named to the *Wisconsin 100* list, which includes the state's 100 largest private businesses, and has been on the list since 1989.
- The *Ideas That Count* program was initiated, awarding associates for coming up with ideas to improve productivity, safety, quality, and reducing costs.
- Keller received its one millionth customer order.

1990 –
- Keller adopted a new corporate identity with a burgundy/black design for its stationery and presentation materials.
- A groundbreaking ceremony was held for the North Park office building, and construction began.
- The first Xerox 5090 unit was installed, and streamlined the workflow for producing guides and manuals.

The children and grandchildren all agree. As grandson Brian said, "It's their money and they can do anything they want with it. Grandma lives and dies for doing things for charities. I don't have a problem with it at all. Without them, I wouldn't have what I have now."

Marne agrees. "They really feel a responsibility to give back. If people knew how much money they have given, I think they'd be shocked, though you certainly wouldn't know it from their lifestyle."

In addition, Marne notes, "They are not content to simply write checks. They want to know the organization, the leader, and their programs. Grandma tries to visit each organization personally. She truly has the spirit of philanthropy and has been my role model."

Downtown office building: 1979

Chapter 11

The Company Today and in the Future

J. J. Keller & Associates, Inc. is what Jack calls a "mud runner," a horse racing term that refers to a horse that moves well even in the muck that follows a heavy rain. In other words, Keller is able to weather difficult economic times while still maintaining its profitability.

"In a strong economy and in a weak economy, we're able to grow our production and sell our products," noted Ron Phillips.

Being conservative, the leadership of Keller didn't want debt to be the albatross around its corporate neck, so it developed a plan to eliminate its debt. In December 1999, the company reached a milestone, paying off its last long-term debt obligation.

"Most companies can't do this. We are in a fortunate position," Ron said. "Nothing crashes a company faster than being beholden to the bank during difficult times. When you have red ink, the bank can call your loan, which can precipitate bankruptcy."

J. J. Keller & Associates, Inc. was able to reach this position by continuing to monitor its capital and operating costs to the point where it did not borrow new money. About five years ago, it even rejected the notion of further expanding its campus by building a new West Park building that would potentially offer needed administrative and/or production space. The economy was quite strong then, but company leaders did not want to take on new debt. "We are very judicious about what we invest in," Ron stated.

Keller Factoid ...

1991 –
- The Keller Foundation, Ltd. was established in honor of Ethel Keller's 70th birthday.
- The North Park office building was completed, and Governor Tommy Thompson attended the dedication.
- K-CAP, the Keller Confidential Assistance Program, began.

1992 –
- A new Komori two-color sheet-fed press was installed to print direct-mail pieces, custom logbook covers, and forms.
- A new feature, PhoneMail®, was added to the telephone system.

1993 –
- The first Novell network was installed, which allowed PCs to connect to the systems.
- The first HP UNIX development system was installed in preparation for the publications conversion which went live in November 1994.

Company Ethics

Ron admires Keller for its company principles. "It's not even a matter of 'we don't violate the laws.' We don't — but through practices and policies, we show that we care about people, care about our customers, and our vendors. We try to be fair, ethical, and not take advantage of any individual or other company."

Ron's words are even more meaningful today because they were said during the 2002 summer of national corporate despair, when seemingly every day there were new reports about corporate scandal. Enron and WorldCom bankruptcies sent chills through the financial world, particularly when questions were raised about accountants who were supposed to protect companies from making costly mistakes, intentional or unintentional.

Ethics in business have never been more important nationally, but these are principles that Keller has always embraced. "The stock market shows that people across the country don't trust the people running companies. A lot of unethical practices are coming out. I believe we are a very ethical company. That's important. Our associates want to be part of a company that makes the right choices," Ron noted.

Bob likes to think of the company as principle-based, but sensitive to other people's beliefs and rights. "We were founded on hard work, innovation, and a passion for customer service, quality, and ethics," he said.

Honored for Service

Paper Industry International Hall of Fame, Inc. award: 2001

In 2001, Jack was inducted into the Paper Industry International Hall of Fame, Inc. This non-profit organization recognizes individuals who have made preeminent contributions to the paper industry worldwide.

Also in 2001, J. J. Keller & Associates, Inc. was given the Wisconsin Association for Career & Technical Education's C.L. Greiber Award of Merit for its contributions to the improvement, promotion, development, and progress of career and technical education in Wisconsin.

The awards for the company that Jack built continue on, including the prestigious Fox Cities Chamber of Commerce's 2002 Manufacturer of the Year Award, which recognizes Keller's leadership in manufacturing and community service.

Keller has also been recognized in other areas:

- Technical Education Champion "TECh" Award from the Wisconsin Technical College District Board Association recognized Keller for its support of Fox Valley Technical College through financial generosity, curriculum assistance, and personnel support.

- International Telly Award, which showcases outstanding commercials, film, and video productions, was presented to Keller seven times for excellence in training videos and music. The honored products include: *Hazard Perception Challenge*, *Extreme 7-Minute Solutions: Mountains*, and *Construction Forklift Training*.

- International AiME Award from the Media Communications Association, which celebrates international excellence in media communications, has recognized Keller for *Extreme 7-Minute Solutions: Mountains* and *Construction 7-Minute Solutions: Hand & Power Tool Safety*.

> **Remember when . . .**
>
> ... it was routine to work Saturdays. On one particular Saturday morning, I greeted Jack Keller as he was coming up the long flight of stairs at the downtown offices and commented about it not being a regular work day. He said, "Son, when you enjoy your work, every day is like a vacation day."
>
> – **Tom Ulrich**
> **Facilities**

- Cameofest Award from the International Television Association has recognized Keller nine times, including a Special Achievement Award in Directing for *Essential Dispatcher Skills*, and a Cameofest Gold for graphic design and animation for *Extreme 7-Minute Solutions: Wind*.

- Wisconsin 100 listing honors the 100 largest privately-held companies in Wisconsin based on annual revenues. Keller has been included on this list for more than 10 years.

- National Safety Council Customer Service Award has been presented to Keller for superior customer service.

A Commitment to Quality

Beyond awards — and at the core of Keller's success — is an unwavering dedication to provide outstanding customer service and quality resources. Keller has a multi-layered system, which includes a total quality management strategic initiatives program, internal and external customer feedback tracking, statistical process controls, and quality assurance sampling from raw materials to finished products.

The results of Keller's quality initiatives are telling. An independent audit of Keller's quality assurance program by the American Red Cross resulted in an overall "meets requirements" rating and a contract award. In addition, on a customer satisfaction survey completed by Dun & Bradstreet, Keller received a Quality of Purchased Product or Service rating of 1.25 on a scale from 1 to 5 where "1" is "exceeds expectations" and "5" is "below expectations."

Keller has also completed the extensive process to become ISO 14001 certified, which means Keller's environmental management system has been evaluated and certified in the areas of operations, documentation, training, communication, operational control, emergency preparedness, preventive and corrective action, records, and internal auditing.

The Associate Principle

At the heart of Keller's strategic planning is retention of quality associates. Why? The individuals who will likely take over for today's leadership team are now hard at work at Keller.

Associate development starts with orientation, continues with mentoring and coaching, and culminates with leadership development training and assistance in career mapping. "We want people to make a career at Keller," Bob said.

All associates are regularly trained on safety and emergency situations, and on topics related to their particular positions. Initially, sales associates are given six weeks of intensive training, followed by continual training on new products, regulatory issues, systems, and selling skills. Also, seminars, conferences, and development sessions are attended on a regular basis by all associates to enhance job performance.

To groom the next generation of leaders, 30 to 40 mid-level managers will participate in a formal leadership development program, which is designed to create the leaders who will

Keller Factoid ...

1994 –
- The new Svecia screen press was installed to print custom labels, door signs, and placards.
- The first six-figure sales order was received from the U.S. Coast Guard with the purchase of 456 guides and 456 three-year subscriptions. The dollar figure was too large to be entered into the computer system.
- The Gain Sharing program began.
- The Keller-Soft® product line was introduced with *Keller-Soft® for OSHA Workplace Safety.*

1995 –
- A Didde-Glaser MLC 17" x 17" 4-color web press was installed in the printing area.
- The first company-developed interactive software product, *Computer-Based Training for OSHA Hazard Communication,* was issued.

Roger Erdmann
32-year associate

Roger Erdmann, manufacturing quality and productivity manager, became a Keller associate in January 1971. He and his brother Roy, who also works at Keller, were boyhood friends of the Keller boys. Roger started as a sheet perforator operator in the bindery, earning $2.50 an hour.

When he was a bindery supervisor, Roger would receive a $10 bonus for each day his group produced 10,000 logbooks. Today, over 90,000 logbooks are produced each day.

Some of Roger's fondest memories include the associate picnics and the Horizon Club events. He also remembers the company using an Erdmann farm tractor to clear snow from the truck bays and parking lots.

Roger says he's stayed with Keller because, "I've always been treated fairly and associates are recognized for their efforts." His decision to assume the quality position in manufacturing was not an easy one to make, but he's very glad he accepted it and enjoys being a part of the success of the manufacturing area.

succeed Bob, Jim, and others now guiding the company. "We are actively looking at succession by forming this leadership development process," Bob said. "We did the same thing 15 to 18 years ago when we brought in a consultant who worked with our managers on leadership development."

One of the reasons for this effort is that the top leaders at the company are in their mid 50s. "We need to develop a succession team," Bob stated. "Rather than replace a president, vice president, or CEO, we need to groom a whole team."

He expects that team to consist of members of the Keller family if they are interested, as well as non-family members — much like the top leaders today are a mix of family and non-family members. The next team will face even more pressure than what exists today, not only because of a more challenging business world, but because J. J. Keller & Associates, Inc. is so attractive to outsiders.

"There's a great demand on a private business from public companies looking at acquisition. We get calls and letters every day," Bob said. "These companies don't want to develop anymore. They want to buy already developed companies."

> **Remember when . . .**
>
> ... all computer entry was completed by the data processing department. They even entered driver trip reports. Any errors were returned to the trip auditor marked in green ink, which was the color assigned to data processing.
>
> **– Dory Santkuyl**
> **Tax & Safety Services**
>
> ... purchase orders were all manually typed.
>
> **– Flo Wall**
> **Procurement**

It is Bob's hope that J. J. Keller & Associates, Inc. stays private. "This company should be in good hands. We have a lot of young folks who are developing nicely," he said.

Retention is important for another reason. "We can't afford turnover." Bob added, "We value our associates' knowledge. When individuals leave, we lose them as assets. We want to hold on to them so we hold on to their knowledge and expertise."

Ron says he has stayed with Keller because he has enjoyed being a part of the growth. "When you are deeply involved with a growing company, you want to be a part of its future successes," he said.

And J. J. Keller & Associates, Inc. has grown. It took 20 years for the company to reach nearly a million dollars in sales — $965,441 in 1973. Ten years later, net sales had grown to $10.5 million and by 1993, sales were more than $50 million. The net sales goal for 2003 is $118 million.

Is there a cap to how much the company can grow? Both Rustin and Marne are quite optimistic. "I think we are just scratching the surface. I don't

When Roy Erdmann, senior web press operator, was home on leave from the Air Force he often helped at Keller assembling books. Upon his discharge, Jim hired him as a press operator in the downtown Neenah building in February 1970. Roy, along with his brother Roger, who also works at Keller, has been friends with the Keller boys since childhood.

Roy recalls that when the production area moved to Vinland, it had to be done quickly. The movers placed a large crane at the back of the downtown building and moved equipment out of window openings. Once the equipment was installed at Vinland, the press operators could finally level their equipment — something that was virtually impossible with the downtown building's old, uneven hardwood floors.

Roy has always enjoyed working with the other associates, recalling that while they seldom took work breaks, they did have some wonderful lunches at Loehning's Restaurant.

Roy operates his press with the intent of providing the highest quality product to his customers — the bindery. He continues to work at Keller because of job security saying, "You can't find another company in the Valley where you can be assured of a job year after year."

Roy Erdmann
33-year associate

Bev Geiger
31-year associate

Bev Geiger, senior staff accountant, began her career at Keller in April 1972 after being interviewed by Bob and Jim. There were just four accounting associates when Bev started and all duties were performed manually. Today, the department has grown to thirty-seven associates in accounting and contracts, records and credit services.

Bev fondly recalls the gatherings after work at "The Old Post Office" on Friday evenings, as well as the annual department Christmas parties. One holiday the group had such a good time at a pre-dinner party, they nearly didn't make it to the restaurant for dinner.

She has seen the tremendous increase and change in the products that Keller sells and recognizes first-hand that putting an emphasis on product development has played an instrumental role in where Keller is today. "The company's emphasis on policies and procedures is also a benefit because it has allowed Keller to grow in a rapid but orderly manner," Bev stated.

One of the reasons she has stayed with the company for thirty-one years is that Keller's growth has given her the opportunity to hold many positions in the accounting area.

see any reason why we can't reach a half-billion dollars in annual sales," Rustin said. Marne agrees. "In terms of growth for the company, the potential is unlimited."

To honor associates who have stayed with the company and contributed to its successes, a recognition group was formed known as the Horizon Club. Rachel Kuhr, who has worked for the company since 1973, was the reason Jack started this group.

Jack and Ethel, who always attended associate events, including the annual women's golf league banquet at George's Steak House in Appleton, were talking with a group of associates, including Rachel. "I had been with the company about five years at the time. Jack kept staring at me as if he didn't know who I was. I was brave enough to say, 'You

Jack acknowledges Rachel Kuhr at the first Horizon Club banquet: 1979

Keller Factoid ...

1996 –
- Keller turned on the switch for a home page on the Internet.
- With the purchase of two imagesetters, prepress was completely remodeled.

1997 –
- The company's first Internet-based product was launched — an online version of the popular newsletter, Keller's *Industrial Safety Report*.
- Keller and the American Trucking Associations formed an alliance, bringing together two former competitors to build on each other's strengths.

1998 –
- Associates began to utilize *GroupWise* for messaging and calendar scheduling.
- A custom-built 11,000-pound, 34-foot long T & B German sheet collator was installed in the bindery to assemble logbooks.

don't know who I am.' I said, 'that doesn't make me feel good. I've worked here five years and you don't know me.' Jack always took pride about knowing all the associates."

The following week she said a flyer came out about a Horizon Club banquet for people who had been with the company for five years or more. At the banquet, Jack gave Rachel credit for the concept of honoring long-time associates with the company. He said he had a hard time recognizing Rachel because she had worked in several different jobs since joining the company. "He never forgot my name after that," she said.

She remembers times following several Horizon Club banquets when Jack would take those who stayed after the dinner to a local nightspot, where the party continued with pizza and drinks until three o'clock in the morning.

Rachel has made her career at Keller because her work continues to be engaging. "This is a very

Sharon Kaddatz, editor of transport operations, came to Keller in February 1973 as a clerk in tax and safety services. Her starting salary was $2.45 per hour. At that time, there were only five associates in the department and they worked in a single office in the downtown building. Now there are over 100 associates.

During those years, the services paperwork process included one sheet of paper for every driver, for every trip. "You can imagine the mountains of paper," Sharon replies. When the first computer was installed in the department, it was a major event.

In the early days, Keller had a very strict dress code and Sharon remembers women being sent home to change when they were dressed inappropriately for the office. She also recalls how surprised she was to learn that a "tractor" didn't refer to a piece of machinery that was used on a farm.

When asked what she likes best about working at Keller, Sharon responds, "Associates are treated very well. We have top-notch working conditions and excellent benefits." She added that the company has always been cautious in their decision-making which she feels is the reason that Keller has never experienced a major staff layoff.

Sharon Kaddatz
30-year associate

Pat Laux
31-year associate

Pat Laux, editor of transport software, was hired in October 1972. She remembers being interviewed by Jack, Bob, and Jim but didn't meet her new boss, George McDowell, until her first day of work. At that time, there were four full-time associates and one part-time associate in the editorial department, which was located in the downtown Neenah building.

As the first elected president of the Horizon Club, Pat remembers how difficult it was to raise money to support their programs. In fact, she recalls selling active wear and other items to raise funds. Today, the company sponsors these associate events.

Over the years, Pat has seen tremendous opportunities for female advancement in the company. She gave the example of Becky Gatza, who started out as an administrative associate and now manages one of the company's largest sales groups. Pat is also impressed that Keller has never had any major layoffs.

Pat is pleased that Keller is giving back to the community that has supported the tremendous growth of the company, saying, "I never thought of leaving Keller for other employment … I enjoy my job and the opportunity to learn something new every day."

interesting business. It challenges your mind all the time," said Rachel, who works in the tax and safety services department. "You don't get bored in this job because you do so many different things."

Jan Reh Hamblin agrees. It's not the same job day after day. As new regulations come out and the company responds, there are always new opportunities to learn and grow as individuals.

"This is a chameleon company. We have worked eight different businesses right here at Keller. We have piloted products and services based on ideas that have come from many of the associates," she said. "The company as a whole has continued to change over and over."

Amy Beirne, who has been with Keller since 1979, remembers being amazed when she joined the company that someone like Gloria Kabke would have stayed in one place for five years. "We're both still here," Amy said with a smile. "I like the constant changing and growing involved with new programs and processes. We've grown so fast and the time has passed so quickly."

Cookie Regal, who has worked in distribution for 27 years, recalls a transition in the public acceptability of working at Keller. "We didn't always have a good reputation. People used to ask, 'You work there?' Now they ask, 'What can I do to get in Keller?'"

Today, there are over 500 Keller associates with more than five years of experience with the company.

Sharing the Wealth

One reason Keller is now a place that many people want to work is its commitment to sharing the wealth and recognizing associates for their efforts. Associates helped make Keller successful and continue to do so, that is why the company has offered a profit sharing and retirement plan since 1974, a 401(k) retirement plan since 1988, plus additional financial incentives for a job well done.

At the time of the profit sharing and retirement plan introduction nearly 30 years ago Jack commented, "We have always thought of our organization as a team with each member doing his best for the team as a whole, as well as for himself. Our profit sharing and retirement plan, as we see it, makes

Dick Roeming, who retired in 1998 as a resale products manager in product development, often tested the quality of potential resale items before they became part of the Keller product line.

One of his favorite tests involved a product that Jack spotted in a catalog called "Truckers' Unstuckers." Dick ordered a set of these four-foot long rubber strips and did a usability test by running his pick-up truck into a snow bank. Sure enough, the Truckers' Unstuckers got him out. Even after this and several other tests proved the product's usefulness, Truckers' Unstuckers were never added to the resale product line!

To test the quality of DOT hazardous materials placards, Dick attached an aluminum "bumper bracket" to the back of his pick-up truck to which he could attach sample placards. These placards happened to have pre-printed four-digit numerals/legends that would correspond to specific hazardous materials — that is, until George McDowell spotted Dick's truck. "That's illegal," George commanded. From then on Dick says, "I would only use placards with the 1203 legend for gasoline. That way, if I was stopped by the highway patrol, I could explain I was carrying a full tank of gas!"

Dick Roeming
retired associate

Keller Factoid ...

1999 –
- Fort Keller at Cub Scout Camp Rokilio, funded by Jack and Ethel Keller, was dedicated.

2000 –
- Bob Keller got "pied" when outbound sales reached $3,000,000 deferred revenue for the year.
- *KellerOnline®* was launched.

2001 –
- The Keller Intranet was launched.
- After three years of preparation, the company received its ISO 14001 certification.

2002 –
- Sales recorded its highest sales year with $105,667,612!
- *Driver Management Online*™ was launched.
- Keller owns twelve registered trademarks.

2003 –
- The 35-acre corporate campus is comprised of 487,000 square-feet of office and plant facilities.
- Jack Keller celebrates his 85th birthday, the company celebrates its 50th anniversary, and Jack and Ethel Keller celebrate 60 years of marriage (in February 2004).

teamwork pay off for you, individually, by increasing old age security and greater piece of mind."

In the first year of the profit sharing and retirement plan, Keller associates shared about $15,000 in profits. It started small but Terry Quirk and Mark Tremble were glad to have it. "My first profit sharing deposit was for $15.10," Terry recalled. "For a family-run company, it was a pretty good profit for that time," Mark added.

Today Keller associates share more than $2 million a year in profits.

Sales associates receive commission on top of their wages, while others participate in the gain sharing program which started in 1994. Under gain sharing, all associates who do not receive incentives or bonuses of any kind are eligible for distributions from the gain sharing fund. Whenever operating profit exceeds 10 percent in any month, a portion of the profit in excess of the 10 percent is set aside to be disbursed to eligible associates on a quarterly basis.

"When I look at J. J. Keller & Associates, Inc., it is not a company of Jack, Bob, and Jim. There are now 950 people who are involved in these efforts and do things that make the company sound and profitable," Ron said. "By and large, it is the combined efforts of a lot of people. I would stack them up against any other company. The strength of our people is the strength of this company."

In a 1998 interview, Bob called the concept of sharing profits with associates, "shared responsibility, shared results." It's just as easy to grow the company as to not grow it, according to Bob. "And these days, you either grow or die."

Remember when . . .

... tax and safety services was located on the mezzanine above data processing. We used the handicap elevator to move our boxes of trip and fuel documents down to the warehouse for storage.

... we had one restroom that wasn't large enough for all the women who worked in the tax and safety services department at that time.

– Robbin Wiley
Tax & Safety Services

A Final Thought

Governor Tommy Thompson, now U.S. Secretary of Health and Human Services, may have described Keller's niche best in 1991 when he came to Neenah to celebrate the opening of its new North Park corporate headquarters. "I know of very few companies that like government regulations, let alone benefit from them," he said. In front of him, he noted, was the exception — J. J. Keller & Associates, Inc.

Jack, Bob, and Ethel with Governor Tommy Thompson at the dedication of North Park: 1991

The company, associates, and facilities have evolved and grown throughout the prosperous 50-year history of J. J. Keller & Associates, Inc.

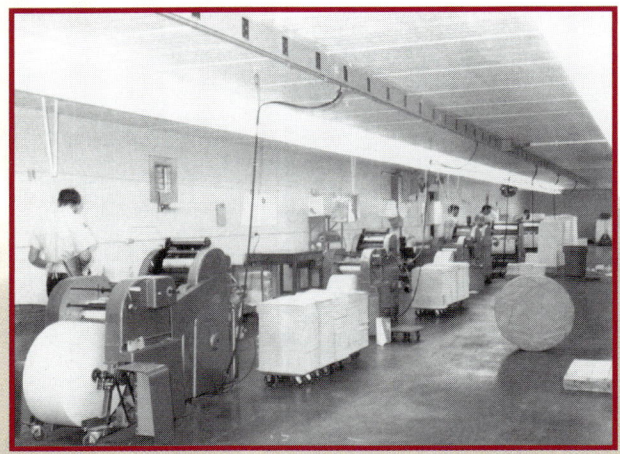
Pressroom: 1972

Jim Keller, production manager: 1972

Signing of first computer contract with NCR: 1972

Company picnic: 1977

Bindery: 1978

First Keller truck: 1980

Recognition for new deferred revenue milestone: 1983

Horizon Club banquet: 1984

Florida trade show: 1985

Corporate operations meeting in the dead animal room: 1986

Jack Keller addressing associates at a recognition luncheon: 1987

Horizon Club bowling event: 1988

Wisconsin 100 celebration: 1989

North Park groundbreaking: 1990

Ribbon cutting for the new North Park building: 1991

Horizon Club award ceremony: 1991

Men's championship softball team: 1993

Horizon Club Packer trip: 1994

George McDowell's retirement party: 1998

Dave Ellis' 50th birthday celebration: 2000

Bob Keller getting "pied" when outbound sales reached $3,000,000 deferred revenue for the year: 2000

Dedication of the Fox Valley Technical College Truck Driver Training Range: 2001

Company poker walk: 2002

Green & Gold Awards Program: 2002

In Memory of Our Associates Who Have Passed Away

Eric Larson 12/23/74	*Debra M. Baldauf* 05/12/95
Harold C. Nelson 04/01/83	*Marcella V. Splinter* 07/22/96
Janice C. Thivierge 11/07/86	*Barbara A. Parsons* 10/10/96
Francis G. Hollenback 08/11/91	*Gregory G. Murray* 11/01/02
Ruth A. Kringel 09/16/91	*Marvin L. Strommen* 01/06/03
Randolph S. Heuer 08/16/93	

Part III
Supplemental Material

Corporate Organizational Activities

After the proprietorship, the corporation was formed in 1958 and carried forward to date. This is a summary of the corporate organization as now established.

Board of Directors

John J. Keller, Chairman

Robert L. Keller, Director

James J. Keller, Director

Ronald M. Phillips, Director

Ethel D. Keller, Director

Marion B. Murvine, Director

John R. Sapp, Corporate Counsel/Interim Director

Shareholders

Shareholders of the corporation include family members, key staff, and management personnel.

Officers

John J. Keller, Chairman (Board of Directors)

Robert L. Keller, President (Chief Executive Officer)

James J. Keller, Executive Vice President (Chief Operating Officer)

Ronald M. Phillips, Senior Vice President - Finance (Chief Financial Officer)

Terence J. Quirk, Senior Vice President - Publications & Products

Mark L. Tremble, Senior Vice President - Sales & Marketing

Ethel D. Keller, Assistant Vice President (Social Services Officer)

Marion B. Murvine, Corporate Secretary/Administrative Officer

John J. Keller
Ethel D. Keller

Robert L. Keller　　　**James J. Keller**　　　**Ronald M. Phillips**

Terence J. Quirk　　　**Mark L. Tremble**　　　**Marion B. Murvine**

Executives

Scott C. Burmeister, Director of Contracts, Records & Credit Services

David R. Ellis, Director of Business Development

Thomas C. Hupf, Director of Information Systems

Anthony M. La Malfa, Director of Human Resource Services

Daniel J. McGraw, Director of Manufacturing

Roger E. Porath, Director of Accounting/Corporate Controller

Webb A. Shaw, Director of Editorial Resources

Thomas J. Cherrier, Corporate Distribution Manager

Raymond L. DuBois, Corporate E-Commerce Marketing Manager

Edward W. Emerick, Corporate Consulting & Educational Resources Manager

Keith D. Keller, Corporate Product Development Manager

Marne L. Keller-Krikava, Corporate Strategic Planning Manager

Robert R. Larsen, Corporate Marketing Manager

Jeffrey P. Lau, Corporate Procurement & Facilities Manager

Janice R. Reh Hamblin, Corporate Special Markets Sales Manager

An Overview of Publication, Product and Service Introductions

1950s

Regulatory Compliance & Service Consulting
Insurance Underwriting for Trucking Companies
Functional Warehousing & Distribution
Interstate Commerce Commission Practice

1960s

Transportation Journal & Exchange Bulletin
Exempt Commodities Guide
Trucking Permit & Tax Bulletin
Trucking Permit Guide
Driver's Daily Log Books

1970s

Contract Carrier Authority Handbook
Common Carrier Authority Handbook
Truck Broker Directory
Emergency & Trip Permit Handbook
Driver Qualification File
Official Driver's Daily Log
Vehicle Sizes & Weights Manual
Monthly Log Summary
Trucking Safety Guide
Keller's Motor Carrier Safety Report
Metric Manual
Metric Guide Series
Federal Motor Carrier Safety Regulations Pocketbook
Hazardous Materials Placards
Hazardous Material Guide: Shipping, Materials Handling, Transportation
Fleet Safety Compliance Manual
Computerized Fuel Tax Reporting Service
Temporary Trip Permits
Driver Log Auditing
Permitting & Reporting
Authority Filings
Safety Consulting
Over-Dimensional Permits
Office/Terminal Inspection for DOT Compliance

1980s

Interstate Commerce Guide
Hazardous Waste Audit Program
Hazardous Waste Regulatory Guide
State Fuel & Mileage Spreadsheet & Forms
Trucker's Almanac
Driver's Technical Handbook
Daily Auto Log
Transportation & Distribution Desk Planner

1980s (continued)

Emergency Response Guidebook
Hazard Communication Guide
Right to Know Training Kit
Trailer Seals
Log Checker®
Driver Training Booklets
Decision Driving Handbook
Driver Videos
Transportation and Distribution Dictionary
Your Daily Log: A Driver's Guide to Hours-of-Service
Driver File-PC Software
Reg-A-Dex®
Hazardous Training Booklets
Canadian Driver's Daily Log
Right to Know Compliance Manual
Shipping Training Booklets
Preparing for the CDL Training Kits
1910 OSHA Guide
OSHA Compliance Manual
Canada/United States Driver's Daily Log
Fleet Tax Compliance Manual
Drug Testing: Motor Carrier Compliance Manual
Keller's Hazardous Materials Transportation Report
Model Driver's Manual
Deregulation Compliance Service Assistance
Hazardous Waste Regulations Seminars
Driver Qualification File Auditing
Vehicle Maintenance Management System
Driver's Log Audit and Management System
Tachograph Log Auditing
Refund Consulting
Technical Support Advisory
OSHA Seminars
Exempt Log Auditing
Field/Technical Support Services

1990s

Chemical Training Booklets
French Language Driver Training Booklets
Truck Licensing, Permitting, and Tax Reporting Seminar
State Hazardous Materials Manual
Hazardous Waste Operations & Emergency Response (HAZWOPER) Compliance
OSHA Part 1926 Construction Safety & Health Compliance
Canadian Truck Licence & Tax Manual
Motor Carrier Safety Standards: Canadian Compliance Manual

1990s (continued)

Emergency Response Guidebook
OSHA Facilities Marking Manual
Transport Border Guide
Annual Vehicle Inspection Label
Lockout/Tagout Safety Training: A Program for Employees
Conspicuity Tape
HM-181: A Driver Training Kit
Training Program for HazMat Employees
Keller's Construction Safety Series
Spill Response Compliance Manual
Vehicle Maintenance: A Comprehensive Guide to Improved Operations & Compliance
Training & Recordkeeping: OSHA/EPA/DOT Crossreference Manual
OSHA for Transportation: Key Compliance Topics
Keller's Maintenance Manager™
Construction Regulatory Guide
Keller-Soft® for DOT Safety
Safety Answer Book: Quick Answers to Your Safety Questions
Hazardous Materials Compliance Manual
Pocket Guide to Hazardous Materials
Keller-Soft® for DOT HazMat Compliance
Keller-Soft® for OSHA Workplace Safety
Fuel Tax Master®
The Logging Solution Series
Forklift Safety: An Operator Training Program
Computer-Based Training
Keller-Soft® Safety Audit Customizer®
Surface Transportation Manual
Written Safety Plans for Construction
Federal Motor Carrier Safety Regulations Motorcoach/Bus Version
Seven-Minute Solutions: Training Videos
MSHA Compliance Manual for Surface Operations
Leader's Guide to Safety Committees
The Straight Truck and Van Driver's Handbook
Keller's OSHA Safety Training Newsletter
Keller-Soft® Transport Policies Customizer®
Keller-Soft® Safety Training Customizer®
Keller's Construction Toolbox Talks
Keller's Office Safety Handbook
Keller-Soft® E-Z Newsletter Customizer®
OSHA Company Policies and Programs
Keller-Soft® for Construction Safety
Practical Behavior-Based Safety
Keller-Soft® Safety Training Customizer®
Keller's Official OSHA Safety Handbook
KellerSCAN® for Log Audit
Keller-Soft® for Food Quality & Safety
Compliance Manual for Food Quality and Safety
Employees Guide to Food Safety
Ergonomics Success Videos

1990s (continued)

Ergonomics: A Step-By-Step Program Developer
Canadian Driver Handbook
Roadside Inspections and DOT Compliance Audits
Keller-Soft® Audit Customizer®
Accident Report Kit with Camera
HACCP Training for Employees- USDA Compliance
HACCP Training for Employees- FDA Compliance
Road Rage Video
Food Safety Video Series
Construction Safety Starter Kit
Scannable Duplicate Logs
KellerSCAN® Log Auditing
Tax Audit Consulting
Drug & Alcohol Random Selection
Paperless Fuel Tax Reporting
Drug & Alcohol File Maintenance

2000s

KellerOnline®
Driver Management Online™
FMLA Manual, Software and Forms
Human Resources Videos
Motorcoach Handbook and Training Solutions
Bilingual Forms
Safety/Security Seals & Supplies
Hazard Perception Challenge Videos
Construction Work Zone Videos
Extreme Seven-Minute Solutions Videos
Medical Exam Form & Certificate
Safe Driver Awards
Keller-Soft® OSHA 300 Recordkeeper
School Bus Driver Videos & Handbooks
HMIS® III Publications, Labels, and Supplies
Motor Vehicle Registration Ordering Service
Electronic KellerScan® Falsification
Transport Security Manual
Cargo Security Training Kit
Regulatory Monitoring & Reporting® Service
Straight Truck Solutions
Labor Law Poster Kits
Human Resources Employee File Packet
Human Resources Value Pack
Hazardous Materials Training Solutions
Transport Security Advisor
Fall Prevention Training for General Industry
Keller-Soft® Safety Talks Customizer®
Keller-Soft® E-Z Access Recordkeeper
Keller-Soft® PowerPoint® Safety Training Customizer®
HazMat Made Easier Handbook
Ready-Mix Vehicle Inspection Forms

Horizon Club

The Horizon Club, founded in 1979 by Jack Keller, was established to honor tenured associates. In the fall of each year, a banquet is held at which time associates who have been with the company for five years are inducted into the club. Further, members who have attained additional five-year milestones are honored. The Horizon Club also sponsors a number of special events throughout the year which are open to all associates. Current members of the Horizon Club include:

Robb L. Aasby
Annette V. Abendroth
Ruth K. Ackerman
Thomas M. Adie
Dee Ann K. Ahrens
Mary E. Albrecht
Jennifer R. Altmann
Donna M. Armstrong
Barbara L. Arndt
Robert W. Atchison
Cindy A. Averbeck
Jeff S. Ayers
Diane M. Baldauf
Crystal R. Barrington
Linda R. Barth
Keri A. Bartman
Robin S. Bastian
Christopher D. Bauer
Susan K. Bauman
Debra J. Bazile
Terry L. Becker
Amy S. Beirne
Mae R. Belongea
Kellie J. Benson
Kristine R. Bergmann
Dave B. Berndt
Bonnie R. Beschta
Angela M. Biesecker
Jean M. Bilitz
Lori A. Binner
Jay J. Birschbach
Erica M. Bitter
Alan R. Blechl
Linda M. Blum
Holly J. Boettcher
Terry M. Bootz Gruett
Linda J. Borree
Kay M. Boss
Lori A. Bourke
Kim M. Branstiter
Melissa F. Brateng
Michael J. Breden
John K. Breese
Rebecca R. Brill
Jayme S. Brooks
Rebecca L. Brooks
Tracy S. Brooks
Todd E. Bruce
Amy S. Bruss
Mark A. Budde
Michael D. Burke
Stacie L. Burton
Timothy S. Busch
Kevin G. Buss
Jeanne M. Callen
David M. Carlsen
Daniel F. Carroll
Joy D. Case
Lori L. Catlin

Mark S. Catlin III
Huichong Chang
Thomas J. Cherrier
James D. Chervenka
Kevin R. Chilsen
Jennifer A. Christie Von Holt
Darlene M. Clabault
Bryan A. Clark
Kim M. Clark
Gail M. Clearwater
Cindy L. Cody
Shelley L. Collins
Melissa S. Coon
Michelle A. Cousineau
Teresa L. Cullum
Sandra J. Cummings
Robert L. Cummins
Melody H. Dallman
Kim L. Daus
Mitchell M. Davidson
Cindy K. Davies
Kimberly D. deBoer
Craig W. Deeg
Susan L. Dehn
Kim K. Delie
Victoria R. Delver
Susan E. Demler
Michael D. Dennee
Lisa R. Dennis
Terry L. Dercks
Deanna M. DeVooght
Patricia A. Dey Olson
Jill A. Diana
Allen W. Ditter
Judith L. Donaldson
Jennifer M. Doran Jung
Larry P. Dorn
Fay A. Dreger
Gregory L. Drews
Stephen E. Du Vall
Kari A. DuBois
Raymond L. DuBois
David B. Duffy
Elizabeth M. Eaton
Lori A. Ebert
Ann M. Ehlers
Lisa C. Ehricke
David R. Ellis
Gary A. Elmer
Edward W. Emerick
Renee K. Engel
Elizabeth J. Engstrom
Roger O. Erdmann
Roy J. Erdmann
Rodney A. Erickson
Shelly R. Etteldorf
Cary T. Farah
Susan M. Farah
Frances Fargen

Michelle R. Fassbender
John R. Felhofer
Valerie S. Fell
Michele A. Fellows
William W. Fenlon
Colleen P. Fink
Marguerite A. Flanigan
Linda S. Forster
Lynn D. Fox
Sherry C. Franson
Sara L. Freeberg
Cheryl E. Freiberg
Pamela M. Fretschl
Beth A. Gallow-Kretkowski
Rebecca L. Gatza
Katherine A. Gaulke
Bryan J. Gawryleski
Chad M. Gehrke
Beverly A. Geiger
Cathy J. Geiger
Sarah E. Gerrity
Connie J. Glasheen
Melanie A. Goetz
Karen H. Gogolewski
Mary M. Goldbeck
Mark R. Goltz
Linda J. Gorman
Michael J. Goss
Charles T. Govin III
Barry M. Grant
Tammy R. Greunke
Gary R. Griesbach
Kara K. Gross
Martin J. Grow
Kelly J. Grutza
Robin L. Gustafson
Lorraine J. Haber
Steven R. Haberkorn
Marcia D. Haedt
Robert C. Halla
Candy A. Hansen
Daren B. Hansen
Perry S. Hansen
Kari L. Hanson
Bernadette M. Hardy-Bomber
Scott B. Harrington
Michael W. Harris
Robert J. Harrison
Vicky L. Hart
Thomas C. Harter
Joan M. Hartjes
Sharon J. Heidke
Michael L. Heimerman
Terry L. Heindl
Marilyn M. Heise
Terri L. Heise
Ryan D. Heller
Terese L. Henry
Nora B. Herbst

Cynthia G. Herman
Heidi M. Hershberger
Sandra K. Hielsberg
Kurt D. Hietpas
Kurt K. Hintz
Kristie L. Hochrein
Tricia S. Hodkiewicz
Mary E. Hoehne
Barbara J. Hoernke
Elroy H. Hoffman
Cheryl J. Holcombe
Steve R. Holcombe
Cindy A. Holschbach
Mary A. Holzer
David J. Hopfensperger
Sally R. Hopton
Debra J. Houts
Glenn L. Huffman
Cynthia A. Hull
Marylou I. Hunter
Thomas C. Hupf
Suzanne P. Ihrig
Kristen M. Jackson
LuAnn K. Jensen
Robert S. Johnson
John R. Jonen
Gloria J. Kabke
Sharon L. Kaddatz
Sara J. Kaminski
LeAnn E. Kaser
Alan B. Kassien
Kurt A. Keberlein
Ethel D. Keller
James J. Keller
John J. Keller
Keith D. Keller
Robert L. Keller
Marne L. Keller-Krikava
William E. Kelly
Phyllis A. Kempf
Sherry L. Kennedy-Brantley
Connie M. Kiel LeMere
Joanne M. Kizewski
Donna M. Klatt
Shannon M. Klatt
JoAnn M. Klavekoske
Carla J. Kline
Julie A. Kloiber
Robert W. Knitt
Mary L. Koch
Jean V. Koehler
Cheryl A. Kohl
Michael J. Kobls
John W. Koslowski Jr.
Corinne A. Kranzusch
Laurie A. Kriese
Amy L. Kriewaldt
Lauri A. Krueger
Kevin R. Kucksdorf

Rachel M. Kuhr
Michael K. Kuphal
Alice J. Kurzynske
Anthony M. La Malfa
Rena R. La Roux
Kreg A. La Rue
Kim F. Laabs
Kim M. Laflin
Patricia K. Lamb
Diane K. Lampert
Richard M. Lang
Michael R. Larsen
Robert R. Larsen
Frances M. Larson
Melissa E. Lasee
Christopher A. Laswell
Jeffrey P. Lau
Janice C. Laubenstein
Sharon A. Lauer
Patricia M. Laux
Debra R. LeBoeuf
James M. Legois
Robert J. Lemke
Steven F. Lemley
Debbie L. Lemon
Troy J. Lentz
Patrick A. Lepinski
Roland R. Leppanen
Kim T. Lewis
Sandra L. Lipina
Harry H. Long
Maria K. Loose
Candy S. Luce
Todd J. Lueke
Leann M. Mader
Nancy A. Marks-McKnight
Kenneth D. Marquardt
Jacqueline K. Marsden
Peggy A. Marta
Billie Jo Mathusek
Karen J. Mauritz
Mary J. Maxwell
Judith M. Mc Donald
Daniel J. Mc Graw
Leanne L. Mc Hugh
Mary B. Mc Kone
Peter M. Mc Laughlin
Diana L. McClone
Sheila L. McClone
Joann L. Meagher
Joy A. Meinen
Mona K. Menning
Tracey L. Merrill
Andrew L. Meyer
Debra S. Meyer
Laura G. Meyer
Ronald D. Meyer
Gregory W. Michael
Tonia A. Micheau
Timothy J. Miller
Lorraine M. Miron
Jody M. Moder
Kim A. Moderson
Carol J. Moffitt
Michael J. Monson
Pamela M. Monson
Jill L. Morin
Mary M. Muellenbach
Judy M. Mueller
Jill M. Murphy
Cheryl A. Murray
Marion B. Murvine
Bruce A. Nelson
Lynn M. Nichols
Julie A. Nussbaum

Robert P. O'Connell
John M. Oblinger
Christine L. Olson
Constance A. Owen
Larry J. Pack
James J. Pahl
Brian D. Pamer
Mary L. Pamer
Lynn M. Parks
Audrey J. Partika
Shelley A. Passehl
David L. Pawelkiewicz
Jacquelyn K. Pederson
Jeffrey J. Peeters
Ann M. Penkala
Bradley T. Penneau
Jeri L. Perschbacher
Amy J. Peters
Julie A. Peters
Wayne E. Peters
Corrina C. Peterson
Timothy J. Peterson
Tina L. Peterson
Greg C. Pettigrew
Cindy J. Pfankuch
Paul T. Philipp
Timothy J. Philipp
Ronald M. Phillips
Wayne T. Phillips
Dorothy P. Piette
John L. Pollack
Roger E. Porath
Donna D. Potratz
Penny A. Pownell
Michael J. Prindle
Mary Teresa Priske
Cory R. Puuri
Terence J. Quirk
Amy L. Radliff
Robert A. Radliff
Karla S. Rajek
Carrie A. Rand
Leslie D. Rasmussen
Cheryl L. Reese
Thelma L. Regal
Janice R. Reh Hamblin
Pamela D. Resnick
Marcia R. Rew
Joe T. Rhoden
Charles D. Richards
Rose M. Ripp
Timothy D. Rippl
Joan A. Roberts
Barbara J. Romnek
Kelly A. Romnek
Cynthia D. Roskom
Randy D. Rowe
Ellen M. Ruffing
Karen A. Ruglio
Stacey J. Ryback
Margaret M. Ryf
Kathy L. Safranski
John H. Sage
Dolores M. Santkuyl
Diane K. Sauer
Kathleen A. Sauer
Daniel J. Sawicki
Sharon L. Schend
Debra L. Schloss
Timmy D. Schmeltzer
David J. Schmit
Sally J. Schmitt
Kathryn J. Schneider
Lori A. Schneider
Jeannette R. Scholl

Judy M. Schreiber
Ruth A. Schroeder
Liane M. Schroth
Todd A. Schudy
Kim A. Schueller
Deborah A. Schultz
Jill M. Schultz
Bradley A. Schulz
Michelle M. Schulz
Keith A. Schwalbe
Barbara A. Schwaller
Kristopher L. Schwartzbauer
Gina C. Seeliger
Theresa M. Segor
Michael T. Shamulka
Webb A. Shaw
Dwight R. Siewert
Randall J. Skoog
Debora J. Slomski
Kevin J. Smerling
Judie G. Smithers
Wendy S. Sommers
Priscilla L. Spielbauer
Susan K. St Pierre
Debra A. Stefanski
Carol J. Stein
Janice R. Steinert
Patricia J. Stelow
Jo Ann A. Sterling
Judith A. Stolzman
Mary C. Strane
Mark H. Stromme
Ann E. Strommen
Jenny S. Stuedemann
Thomas P. Subert
Michael A. Svoboda
Dean J. Sweere
Jennifer J. Taber
Jill E. Taylor
Vinita M. Tellock
Randel J. Thome
Trevor A. Thompson
Marilyn J. Tiede
Paula C. Todd
Frances A. Tokarski
Glenn W. Tollar
David A. Tooley
Carmelo G. Trejo
Mark L. Tremble
Thomas G. Ulrich
Tammy L. Valdez
Judy A. Van Dyke
Kevin J. Van Dyn Hoven
Beverly R. Van Geffen
Elizabeth A. Van Handel
Lisa A. Van Hulst
Christopher S. Van Rooy
Tracey M. Van Stippen
Sandra K. Vanden Boogaard
Julie A. Vanden Boom
Amy J. Vanden Oever
Tana R. Vandenberg
Carla J. Vanderheyden
Richard V. Velpel
Steven W. Velpel
Judy A. Wadel
Bonnie A. Wagner
Vanessa K. Wagner
Florine Wall
Cynthia A. Ward
John J. Watters
Brenda L. Weber
Betty J. Weiland
Linda S. Wereley
Gretchen M. Westphal

Nancy A. Wetmore-Simons
Robert J. Whitney
Shari M. Wickesberg
Duane A. Wiedmeyer
Bonnie L. Wieseke
Thomas D. Wildermuth
Robbin Jo Wiley
Beth A. Will
Bonnie L. Williams
Joel A. Williams
Todd B. Williams
Zita M. Williams
Debra S. Wilson
James E. Wilson
Patrick A. Wilson
Timothy B. Wilson
Kim I. Winter
Linda J. Witkowski
Charles L. Witt
James R. Witt
Janet M. Witthuhn
Gerald L. Woodson
Donna M. Wunderlich
Catherine M. Wunrow
Michele L. Yahr
Pamela J. Yonke
Angela M. Zak
Jennifer M. Zanders
Patricia J. Zastrow
Amy L. Zemlock
Richard L. Ziebell
Thomas J. Ziebell
Mark A. Zimmerman
Lisa A. Zwickey

Retiree Listing:

Joan M. Abraham
Betty J. Backman
Gloria A. Bauer
Constance G. Bayer
Marie E. Beede
Catherine J. Clark
Barb L. Dickow
Betty J. Doud
Barbara A. Fitzgerald
Fern L. Fuhrmann
Martha J. Hildebrand
Thomas J. Hollenback
Shirley K. Horn
Gerri B. Karnopp
Ervin F. Koch
Dee M. Koszalinski
Jeanette K. Lucas
George B. McDowell
Patricia E. Miller
Kendall A. Parker
LaVera M. Peterson
John E. Poris
Richard L. Roeming
Patricia A. Schmidt
Karen L. Smith
Lila Stenner
Gertrude A. Van Linn
Jane E. Wysocki

Honorary Member:

E. Munroe Hjerstedt

Philanthropic Activities

The Keller Foundation, Ltd. was established in 1991 in honor of Ethel Keller's 70th birthday. Substantial funding has been contributed to the foundation by John and Ethel Keller.

The John J. & Ethel D. Keller Donor-Advised Fund at the Community Foundation for the Fox Valley Region, Inc. was established in 1994. The Kellers have made substantial donations to this fund.

Further, it should be noted that the estate of Jack and Ethel, beyond allocation of personal assets to family members, is assigned to the Keller Foundation, Ltd. after death. Also, activities of both the Keller Foundation, Ltd. and the Donor-Advised Fund at the Community Foundation will continue into the future. A program is in place to provide for management by the Keller family and administration by the corporate staff, with support provided by members of the Community Foundation.

To date, some of the major projects that have been funded include:

- Fort Keller at Camp Rokilio, a Boy Scout camp in Keil, and the volunteer center and naturalist area for the Boy Scout Center in Appleton
- Starship Discovery exhibit at the Fox Cities Childrens Museum in Appleton
- Establishment of the Emergency Medical Fund at the Community Clinic in Appleton
- Volunteer center and outdoor courtyards at the Fox River Area Girl Scout Center in Appleton
- Truck driving range at Fox Valley Technical College in Appleton
- Courtyard at Lutheran Homes in Oshkosh
- Elevator at Monte Alverno Retreat Center in Appleton
- Two courtyards at Park View Health Center in Winnebago
- Village library in Plainfield
- High school at Rawhide Boys Ranch in New London
- Early Childhood Center at St. Gabriel Parish in Neenah
- Trauma Center Room at Theda Clark Medical Center in Neenah
- Major funding toward the construction of the Winneconne Civic Center

Concluding Remarks

With any complex operation established and functioning over a 50-year period, it is obvious that from its founding to date, the attitude for success goes beyond the founder who may be alive at the 50-year anniversary or long gone.

As an operation that started with one professional and one associate (wife Ethel) with later growth to an approximate 950 staff level with direct, contract, and professional support, it is obvious that the corporation has not only occupied a good place in the economy, but has had reasonable growth and success with allowances for continual progress through acquirement of adequate staff personnel.

For example, when the boys were in high school, they were conferred with as to possible careers with the company. They were advised that if they were willing to go along, the company would expand to accommodate that growth. Both Bob and Jim stated that they wanted lifetime careers with the organization and so our expansion continued.

Ethel, the first associate, handled the home-front until the boys entered college, after which she joined the organization. In fact, she established our world-class technical library which is one of the finest of its kind — a terrific asset supporting our success.

Bob started with the company at age 12 and is now President and Chief Executive Officer. He is a graduate of the University of Wisconsin-Oshkosh with a degree in economics. Bob and his wife, Lynne, have four children and four grandchildren:

- Marne and her husband, Alec and children — Marne currently serves as Corporate Strategic Planning Manager for the corporation.

- Rustin and his wife, Christina — Rustin currently serves as Internet Product Manager for the corporation.

- Rachael and her husband, Philip and children — Rachael is a primary school teacher.

- Adam operates an Internet-based reptile cage business.

Jim started at age 12 and is now Executive Vice President and Chief Operating Officer. He is a graduate of Madison Technical College with a degree in graphic arts. Jim and his wife, Rosanne, have two children:

- Brian and his wife, Melissa — Brian currently serves as a Programmer and Melissa as a Printed Publications Training and Program Specialist.

- Angela currently attends Fox Valley Technical College in Appleton.

Tom worked for the corporation for a number of years. He attended college in Oshkosh where he majored in biology. After several years in the military, Tom was incapacitated due to ill health. He remains in good spirits and also is a large shareholder in the corporation.

Beyond the family, a very large group of men and women have contributed greatly to our success. All the personnel in the organization are administratively, technically, or professionally trained which is unusual for a complex group of our size.

It should be reiterated that the company operates on the associate principle created by myself. This unique principle allows all associates to function fully with their assignments at whatever level of responsibility assigned to assure adequate performance and results. In our experience, this has resulted in a successful operation and has particularly allowed us to retain those individuals who substantially contributed to the overall success. To our knowledge, we are the only organization within our scope of national and international activities operating on the associate principle plan. Undoubtedly, this has greatly contributed to our current debt-free position.

At this time, it also should be stated that I personally did not contemplate that I would reach the age of 85, that I would be married for 60 years, and that I would remain chairman of a 50-year-old organization. It is heart-warming to not only look back but also forward to the future with our family and associates, allowing for continued success.

God bless the corporation, our family, our associates, the state, the nation, and the world.

John J. Keller

John J. Keller
Founder & Chairman